Supermax Prisons: Beyond the Rock

Donice Neal, Editor

American Correctional Association
Lanham, Maryland

Mission

The American Correctional Association provides a professional organization for all individuals and groups, both public and private, that share a common goal of improving the justice system.

Cover design by Capitol Communication Systems, Inc., Crofton Maryland.
Cover photos courtesy of Capitol Communication Systems, Inc., Crofton Maryland.

Printed in United States of America by Magnet Print Brokers, Alexandria, Virginia.

ISBN: 1-56991-163-0

This publication may be ordered from:
American Correctional Association
4380 Forbes Boulevard
Lanham, Maryland 20706-4322
1-800-222-5646, ext.1860

For information on publications and videos available from ACA, contact our worldwide web home page at: http://www.aca.org

Supermax prison: beyond the Rock/Donice Neal, editor.
    p.cm.
    Includes bibliographical references and index.
    ISBN 1-56991-163-0 (pbk. : alk. paper)
        1. Prisons--United States. 2. Prison administration--United States. I. Neal, Donice.

HV9649.S88 2002
365'.973--dc21

Table of Contents

Foreword by James A. Gondles, Jr., CAE...*v*

Chapter 1: Supermax Prisons: Why?...1
Thomas J. Stickrath, J.D. and Gregory A. Bucholtz, Ph.D.

Chapter 2: Building a High-Security Prison...15
Nolin Renfrow

Chapter 3: Developing the Mission and Goals...29
James D. Hart

Chapter 4: Staffing a Supermax Prison..37
James M. Greco

Chapter 5: Technology and the Supermax Prison..53
Donice Neal

Chapter 6: Use of Force in the Supermax Prisons: Setting the Example........67
Eugene E. Atherton

Chapter 7: Inmate Incentive Programs..85
James H. Bruton

Chapter 8: Managing Violence in Supermax:
    A Discussion of Research Findings and Their Application to
    Reducing Violence in Supermax Institutions and Beyond........................99
Jerald Justice, M.S.W and Myla Young, Ph.D.

About the Authors...119

Index...123

Foreword

The forerunner of today's supermax prisons is the notorious Alcatraz prison, known as "The Rock." From 1934 to 1963, the prison housed the federal government's most violent and difficult-to-manage inmates. This concentration model was abandoned, however, during the 1960s. After an increase of violence against staff and prison unrest, the federal government developed a high-security control unit at the U.S. Penitentiary in Marion, Ohio, in 1983. Marion housed the government's most violent inmates until it opened the Administrative Maximum Penitentiary in Florence, Colorado, in 1994.

Faced with an increasing number of violent offenders, many states have developed supermax prisons to isolate and control these difficult offenders from the general population. As Reggie Wilkinson, director of the Ohio Department of Rehabilitation and Correction, notes, "Many of us have determined that removing predatory and other dangerous offenders from the population improves safety and security systemwide. . . . Segregation cells in other facilities can be used more effectively when not clogged by repeat offenders . . . the 'supermax facilities' become a disincentive for seriously negative behavior."

Supermax Prisons: Beyond the Rock provides an A to Z review of supermax prisons in the United States today. Topics range from planning and designing the prison to providing staffing and programming. We hope that this publication provides correctional staff and criminal justice students with a comprehensive understanding of the purpose and operations of supermax prisons.

James A. Gondles, Jr., CAE
Executive Director
American Correctional Association

Chapter 1: Supermax Prisons: Why?

Thomas J. Stickrath, J.D.
Assistant Director
Ohio Department of Rehabilitation and Correction
Columbus, Ohio

Gregory A. Bucholtz, Ph.D.
Assistant Chief Inspector
Ohio Department of Rehabilitation and Correction
Columbus, Ohio

As I walked among these solitary cells, and looked at the faces of the men within them, I tried to picture to myself the thoughts and feelings natural to their condition. I imagined the hood just taken off, and the scene of their captivity disclosed to them in all its dismal monotony.

Charles Dickens on Eastern State Penitentiary, 1842

Introduction

The state of corrections in the United States has changed dramatically since the beginning of the Eastern State Penitentiary's solitary reform ideology. However, many of the basic tenets associated with this style of incarceration continue to be debated due to the expanding use of the "supermax" prison. Despite a philosophical change—from one of reform toward one of management—some would say that the effects of isolation on inmates during the nineteenth century parallel today's segregated housing units and facilities. The strong Quaker influence within the early Pennsylvania system fostered the belief that solitary confinement (with its absence of internal and external contact) would allow inmates to reflect on their crimes, thus hastening repentance.

In contrast, today's supermax prison is founded on management principles that reflect the need to isolate inmates due to a variety of safety and security concerns. Such concerns frequently involve:

- the nature of the current offense(s) and its notoriety
- repetitive assaultive or violent institutional behavior
- threats of escape or actual escape
- the inciting or threat to incite disturbances in a correctional facility

The concept of maintaining a "prison within a prison" is certainly not new to corrections. Isolating inmates from the general prison population in special housing or management units for disciplinary reasons has undoubtedly been in existence since the development of prisons in America. For example, the New York State Prison at Auburn used a variety of disciplinary sanctions that included prisoner separation into small individual cells. Similarly, the Eastern State Penitentiary used a dungeon cellblock for inmates who violated prison rules. Today, some form of segregation exists in nearly every prison. However, what has differentiated the supermax prison from the traditional disciplinary unit found in most prisons concerns the extended timeframe or, in some instances, the permanency of the segregation.

Historically, many correctional systems have tried to manage predatory and other high-risk inmates in different ways, including dispersal, concentration or consolidation, and isolation (Hershberger, 1998; Thigpen, 1999). The concept of dispersal is perhaps the most frequently used approach to managing troublesome inmates. Typically, these problematic inmates are administratively transferred to another facility within a state system; the process may also involve increasing the security level for these offenders. Occasionally, dispersal may involve the Interstate Compact Agreement, whereby inmates are housed within another jurisdiction (the compact "governs the travel, movement, and supervision of adult probationers or parolees from a sending state, where they have been convicted of crimes, to a receiving state," National Institute of Corrections, July 23, 2002). The concept of dispersal is probably best illustrated by one of the responses to the growing security threat group and gang problem in correctional systems. Some jurisdictions use a circuit-type system in which active gang members or leaders are not allowed to spend a significant amount of time in one particular facility. They are continuously transferred in an attempt to disrupt their efforts to develop a unified organization and increase their membership base.

As prison populations grew in the 1990s, and crowding reached record levels, the process of dispersal became more complex. Agencies were confronted with an increasing number of high-risk, predatory inmates that was not proportionate to the number of available beds. Dispersal continues to be the common way of handling offenders with problem behaviors. However, the use of a concentration or consolidation approach to managing these inmates has grown dramatically. Many correctional systems are now operating high-security prisons that are used exclusively for housing problem inmates. These systems believe that removing and isolating high-risk, predatory inmates enable staff to manage general population offenders more effectively. *Simply concentrating high-risk offenders into a single unit or facility, however, does not, in itself, lead to safer and more effective inmate management.*

Concentrating the most volatile inmates without implementing increased security measures could exacerbate the management problems that initially led to the need for consolidation. Because these offenders have already exhibited disruptive and predatory behavior—either within the general population or in segregation—cell isolation and strict limitations on movement and contact have become common practices in these facilities.

Some critics suggest, however, that inmate placement into high-security environments such as a supermax facility does not occur because of actual behavior. Rather, placement is based on either predicted future behavior or suspected group membership (Toch, 2001). This belief is perhaps best exemplified in the Human Rights Watch report on Virginia's Red Onion State Prison. The report maintained that many inmates were placed in supermax security confinement based solely on the length of their sentence (Human Rights Watch, 1999). In many jurisdictions such as Ohio, however, placement criteria are restrictive and based on past behavior that occurred either internally or externally to its state system.

Historical Development

As we discussed earlier, the placement of inmates into high-custody, controlled environments has a long history within the United

States. But the historical development of prisons now commonly referred to as "supermax" can be traced to 1934 when Alcatraz became the high-security penitentiary for the federal prison system. Alcatraz opened in 1934 to house the federal government's "most highly publicized offenders, its most sophisticated escape artists and riot leaders, and its most assaultive inmates" (Riveland, 1999). It operated during the post-Prohibition and post-Depression period in America. After the prison closed in 1963, the Federal Bureau of Prisons did not use the supermax concept (indefinite administrative segregation) until converting the U.S. Penitentiary in Marion, Illinois in 1983. Today, most of the sixty or more supermax prisons in operation in the United States use the total lockdown philosophy developed at Marion.

The era of rehabilitation in corrections and high operating costs eventually led to the closing of Alcatraz in 1963. The federal government abandoned the idea of concentrating hard-to-manage inmates and dispersed them to prisons across the country.

However, an increase in violence and assaults toward staff led the federal government to establish a high-security control unit at the U.S. Penitentiary in Marion, Illinois in 1978. After the deaths of two officers and an inmate in 1983, Marion was converted to indefinite administrative segregation or lockdown. The prison housed the federal government's most violent and troublesome inmates until the opening of the Administrative Maximum Penitentiary in Florence, Colorado in 1994.

Many states have housed their most violent inmates in one or more prisons, but they have seldom operated routinely on total lockdown. Even maximum-security prisons usually allow inmate movement, interaction, and work. Today, however, most of the sixty or more supermax prisons in operation in the United States use the total lockdown philosophy as a method of controlling today's violent and disruptive inmates.

The reasons for the proliferation of supermax prisons in America are twofold. First, many correctional systems have been confronted with crowding due to the increasing inmate population and the influx of drug offenders, gang members, mentally ill, and young offenders. To maintain order, these systems have chosen to isolate the most disruptive inmates from the general population. Some officials state that their supermax prisons also act as a deterrent for some offenders who might be prone to disruptive behavior.

Second, supermax prisons are politically and publicly attractive. They are symbols that a state is getting "tough on crime."

Why Supermax?

I. Institutional Management

The management of inmates raises a number of complex issues involving the provision of services, the maintenance of safety and, where appropriate, the use of sanctions. To effectively manage inmates, staff usually identify, classify, and monitor disruptive offenders based on their exhibited behaviors—either prior to or during incarceration. However, defining which behaviors constitute a disruptive label is difficult due to the extensive number of possible scenarios in which offenders can be involved. Correctional managers would be remiss in attempting to categorize a multitude of behaviors into some type of a checklist that would isolate specific actions. Doing so inevitably would result in numerous overclassifications and false-positive generalizations, thereby creating a management dilemma.

Most, if not all, correctional systems use various standardized criteria to determine which inmates pose a substantial security risk. However, final decisions for supermax placement are typically determined on a case-by-case basis.

For example, the Ohio Department of Rehabilitation and Correction established its criteria for potential supermax placement within departmental policy. As in many states, placement into Ohio's high maximum security occurs through the inmate classification system. It is similar to placement into any security classification, with several levels of review and an opportunity for inmates to appeal their recommended upgraded status. In Ohio, all of the following assignment criteria must be present before an inmate can be recommended for placement at the Ohio State Penitentiary:

1. The inmate is or is about to be classified as maximum security;
2. the inmate presents the highest degree of threat to the security and order of the department and its institutions in the professional judgment of the classifying official; and
3. the inmate has demonstrated behavior that meets high maximum-security criteria, as defined as meeting any of the following:

   a. The inmate's conduct or continued presence at his current institution poses a serious or chronic threat to the physical safety of any person, or to the security of the prison;
   b. the nature of the inmate's criminal offense indicates that the inmate poses a serious or chronic threat to the physical safety of any person, or to the security of the prison;
   c. the inmate has participated in, has threatened to participate in, or is encouraging a disturbance or riot;
   d. the inmate has conspired to introduce contraband that may pose a serious threat to the security of the prison;
   e. the inmate functions as a leader or enforcer of a security threat group;
   f. the inmate poses a serious threat of escape; or
   g. the inmate has demonstrated an ability to compromise the integrity of staff.

Not surprisingly, the types of behavior constituting potential assignment into a lock-down environment such as a special management housing unit or supermax facility is strikingly similar across all states. Despite a wide variance between jurisdictions on the definition of supermax (Riveland, 1999), most use similar, specific behaviors and types of associations when recommending inmate placements into supermax confinement.

Criteria for placement consideration generally include: committing violent assaults against staff and other offenders, making a serious escape threat, being a gang leader or enforcer, and trying to have substantial quantities of drugs smuggled or conveyed into a prison. In some states, such as Virginia, sentence length also is taken into account. The criteria used by correctional systems are presented only as a guideline for use in determining the most appropriate inmate classification assignments.

A small number of inmates may exhibit behavior that has an impact directly and/or indirectly on the stability of operations. Therefore, the potential risk lends support for separating the inmates from the general population. In fact, it could be argued that this concept has been the premise for segregation units since their inception. When particular behaviors threaten the very fabric of a facility's security, then the facility must attempt to reestablish the parameters governing its correctional management. Traditionally, jurisdictions have generally addressed the problem by using special management or housing units that isolate inmates for a definite period of time spanning either a couple of days or several months. By design, these units are located within the exiting facility where the behavior occurred. Spatial differentiation from the general population, thereby, is minimal.

Interestingly enough, a plethora of literature states that increased spatial differentiation leads to further complexity within an organization (Robbins, 1990). But the opposite is true within a correctional setting. Housing the "worst" inmates in the institution—where they have committed their violent or predatory behavior and have placed themselves in a status position—clearly can foster additional disruption within the general population, albeit indirectly. The state of Ohio is a prime example of this phenomenon.

Prior to the opening of Ohio's supermax prison, the Ohio State Penitentiary (OSP), the most violent, predatory inmates were housed at its lone maximum-security prison, the Southern Ohio Correctional Facility. One of the leading forces behind the movement for a stand-alone "supermax" facility was the 1993 Easter riot at the Southern Ohio Correctional Facility. Inmates housed at this facility and at others around the state perceived the maximum-security facility to be as easy to disrupt as any facility in the state. Spatially, the inmates who were housed in the special management unit continued to be geographically connected to the general population. Communication between segregation and the general population, therefore, was not necessarily controlled nor eliminated. After the eleven-day siege (Wilkinson and Stickrath, 1997), the need to separate inmates based on their disruptive behavior became paramount to the successful operation and management of the state's entire correctional system so that future riotous behavior could be minimized. If anything, the riot showed that special management housing units located within high-security prisons were not a panacea for the security risks posed by violent, predatory inmates.

Many facilities apply the supermax philosophy to special management units located within a multilevel secure prison (for example, Pelican Bay State Prison). Yet, the ability to manage the "worst of the worst" becomes more complex due to the lack of spatial differentiation. The need for further distance between inmates identified as disruptive and those who conform to the rules and policies but are vulnerable to being influenced becomes a critical task for management. As a logical step, correctional administrators, as well as legislative bodies, have moved forward with the design and subsequent construction of stand-alone supermax prisons.

Reginald Wilkinson, director of the Ohio Department of Rehabilitation and Correction, summarizes the need for supermax prisons:

"Many of us have determined that removing predatory and other dangerous offenders from the population improves safety and security systemwide. By developing 'supermax' prisons, we can isolate problem offenders in one facility. While this concept has come under some criticism, the benefits appear to outweigh perceived problems. Recalcitrant offenders participate in targeted in-cell programming rather than sitting idle in a disciplinary cell. Supermax staff receive specialized training in working with dangerous prisoners, and policies and procedures are specific to problem offenders without restricting the privileges of the general population. Segregation cells in other facilities can be used more effectively when not clogged by repeat offenders, and finally, the 'supermax' facilities become a disincentive for seriously negative behavior. Further, technological advancements have made high security more 'user friendly'" (Wilkinson and Stickrath, 1997).

II. Operational Security

The overriding justification for the use of a supermax philosophy is rooted in the need for security. In virtually every case, inmate placement into this type of environment has rested on past behaviors, either "on the street" or during their incarceration. Actual disruptive behavior, however, may not necessarily identify those inmates most threatening to the safety and security of an institution. Take, for example, a known prison gang leader who may have a "clean" conduct report history but who instructs others to commit violations. For traditional classification systems (which contain either static or dynamic/changeable) measures of inmate behavior, the gang leader most likely will score at a decreased security level despite being a serious security threat. Actual behavior, therefore, cannot in and of itself be the lone criteria for determining whether a particular inmate is a risk to security.

Sometimes, intelligence gathered both internally and externally to the correctional system helps identify inmates for supermax placement. Internally, security threat group teams, telephone and mail monitoring, and inmate informants are used to prevent potential security problems. External intelligence gathered sometimes also can result in a temporary supermax placement for inmates. Other criminal justice organizations, such as law enforcement, prosecutors, and judges, often provide correctional departments with information that indicates particular inmates present a danger to security. This information may be based on professional judgment and/or known established behaviors committed in the community (which are not recorded in a presentence investigation or other document in an inmate file). However, supermax placement solely due to information provided by other agencies is rare. Yet, it does present itself as one of the proactive mechanisms available to combat potential security risks.

Similar to law enforcement, change in correctional agencies is generally reactive rather than proactive when it pertains to security. As unique experiences, dilemmas, or crises arise, administrators implement changes to reduce their reoccurrence. Unlike law enforcement, however, prisons are not an extension of society at large where a majority of the behavior exhibited in the community is predictable. Predictability in behavior is seen as the underlying factor that maintains a balance between the enforcement of laws and policies and the rights of citizens (Langworthy and Travis, 1999). The mere purpose of incapacitation signifies that the behaviors of persons sentenced to prison are unpredictable. Inmates already have demonstrated an inability to abide by the laws of society. Thus, there is no reason to believe that their behavior would significantly change in a confined environment where everyone has committed criminal acts—often despite efforts to rehabilitate the inmates. The large variation in recidivism rates across all jurisdictions illustrates this phenomenon. It is well established that one of the best predictors of future behavior is past behavior.

Even though inmates' past behavior is important, classification decisions in a supermax setting continue to be determined on a case-by-case basis. This individual assessment occurs because of the possible mitigating and aggravating circumstances surrounding a particular event or pattern of behavior. As shown in Table 1, some of the examples presented could, at face value, be easily placed into the opposite decision category.

Inmates identified as posing the greatest risk to security (as determined by both institutional and administrative staff) traditionally were transferred to special management housing units within a preexisting prison. They are now being placed into stand-alone supermax facilities where they exist. Philosophically indistinguishable from one another, special management housing units and stand-alone supermax prisons both use a concentration approach to managing high-risk, high-security inmates. As we previously discussed, the movement toward inmate concentration continues to pale in comparison to the use of dispersal for problem inmates. This situation is simply due to the vastly smaller percentage of inmates identified as predatory and high-risk.

Concerns about operational security extend not only to the general populations within each prison but also to the manner in which inmates are housed in a supermax facility. Removing the most volatile inmates from the general population and segregated units of an institution is fundamental to maintaining order and safety for inmates and staff alike. Statistics on assaultive behavior within segregation units shows that they do not inhibit violence despite their punitive nature. For example, data on inmate-on-staff assaults in Ohio from 1996-2000 show that, on average, 41.1 percent of all assaults occurred in segregation. Conversely, only 1.8 percent of all inmate-on-staff assaults in calendar year 2000 occurred at Ohio's high maximum-security prison. Recent national figures also suggest that the average number of assaults against staff per agency increased to their highest

Table 1.   Examples of Approvals and Denials to Ohio State Penitentiary

Approvals

1. Inmate considered extreme escape risk by Secret Service and FBI. Inmate has access to millions of dollars and is affiliated with terrorist group. Offered an inmate 1 million dollars to kill another inmate who testified in his trial.
2. Placement per request of Southern Regional Director. Inmate is believed to have been involved in smuggling a gun into an institution. Inmate has also been threatening staff.
3. Conspired with aunt to have crack brought into institution. Inmate offered money to correction officer to bring in drugs. Aunt provided money and drugs to undercover State Highway Patrol Officer to bring drugs into institution.
4. Inmate smuggled cocaine into an institution and sold it on compound. In 1991, inmate seriously assaulted a food service staff member who caught inmate engaged in a sex act with another inmate.
5. Inmate involved in threats against witnesses from prison. Investigation showed inmate establishing himself in security threat group leadership role and observed other inmates providing security. Believed to be the leader of X-Clan gang who intimidated witnesses in his criminal case. Believed to be involved in a number of murders in Columbus.
6. Inmate caught in escape plot by sending out a map containing pick-up points. Plot also verified in monitoring of telephone call.
7. Inmate found in possession of two ounces of marijuana, materials for hooch production, and instructions for the monitoring and installation of the institution's perimeter camera system.

Denials

1. Inmate attempted to smuggle one ounce of marijuana during a visit.
2. Inmate found in possession of a shank. Institution claims that the inmate is a leader in Aryan Brotherhood. Central Office security threat group maintains that inmate does not qualify as high maximum security.
3. In possession of a shank (small spear) and toothbrush shank. Inmate also threw urine on staff.
4. Conspired to attempt to escape while out to court. Inmate claimed in a letter and during telephone calls to be in possession of a handcuff key. Asked family members to be at court. No handcuff key found on inmate.
5. Inmate came off of a wall swinging and kicking at correction officers. One officer was kicked and another hit.
6. Inmate found to have been committing repeated telephone harassment.
7. Inmate committed self-mutilation, attempted to establish a relationship with staff member, masturbated, and broke toilet in cell.

Table 2. Percentage of Inmate-on-Staff Assaults in Ohio by Location 1996-2000

Location of Assault	1996	1997	1998	1999	2000	Avg.
Segregation Units	48.1	44.8	39.3	37.4	36.0	41.1
General Population	22.7	25.1	28.2	25.9	32.3	26.8
Residential Treatment Units	6.8	9.2	8.1	6.5	7.9	7.7
Food Service Area	6.6	3.4	6.1	5.1	5.1	5.3
Corridor/Hallway	3.6	4.6	4.7	3.6	3.6	4.0
Compound Yard	2.6	2.6	2.4	4.2	2.1	2.8
Infirmary	2.6	1.1	2.6	3.2	2.7	2.4
Recreation Building/Yard	0.4	2.5	2.2	3.0	2.1	2.0
High Maximum Unit	na	na	na	6.1	1.8	1.6
Other Area	6.6	6.7	6.4	5.0	6.4	6.3

Source: Bureau of Research, Ohio Department of Rehabilitation and Correction

level in 1999 to 367 from a low of 220 in 1992 (Camp and Camp, 2000). In most jurisdictions, segregation is considered a temporary housing placement where an inmate will spend a defined period of time before being returned to the general population.

Because segregation is temporary, inmates who repeatedly violate policies and procedures find themselves moving back and forth between the general population and segregation. Frequent placement in segregation does not necessarily result in a supermax placement unless the behavior warrants such a move. However, significant security concerns are raised when an inmate exhibiting either assaultive, violent, or predatory behavior remains at the institution where the behavior originally occurred. Assaults on staff, for example, can increase the status of an inmate with his peers in the general population, thus increasing the likelihood of continued security concerns.

Using a dispersal approach to house inmates who have met a jurisdiction's criteria for supermax placement would only result in displacing the inmates from one prison to another. The net effect on a reduction of security concerns would be zero. Using a concentration approach to managing the "worst of the worst" offenders improves the security of the other facilities within the prison system. But security concerns become most pronounced with the housing of these inmates in a supermax setting. Unfortunately, maintaining a general population environment for inmates who have exhibited a level of behavior that has seriously jeopardized the safety and security of a prison would be impractical. Therefore, inmates confined to a supermax facility are placed in a single-cell, isolated atmosphere where movement is highly restricted and limited.

Security versus Mental Health

One of the most pressing concerns and criticisms about the operation of supermax prisons is the use of and reliance on cell isolation. Based on the model developed at the U.S. Penitentiary at Marion and, more recently the Colorado State Penitentiary, inmates are frequently confined to their cells twenty-two to twenty-three hours per day. Aside from the need for supermax prisons, the effects of solitary confinement on the mental health of inmates is perhaps the most controversial topic debated about the prisons.

The topic had been mostly limited to debate among mental health professionals. But it is emerging in the literature as a key issue in scrutinizing and defending correctional practices through empirical findings. However, despite the movement from anecdotal case studies to empirical analyses through the use of experimental and longitudinal research designs, the conclusions being drawn remain somewhat tenuous. Depending on which side of the argument one takes, studies exist to support that belief. For example, studies have found that solitary confinement in prison is neither universally damaging, aversive, or intolerable (Suedfeld, Ramirez, Deaton, and Baker-Brown, 1982) nor psychologically detrimental. Differences did not exist between segregated and nonsegregated inmates on a number of psychological inventories (Zinger and Wichmann, 1999). Conversely, other studies have shown solitary confinement to have severe psychological effects on inmates (Grassian, 1983; Grassian and Friedman, 1986; Hodgins and Cote, 1991).

Some would argue that incarceration creates psychological effects that include depression, anger, anxiety, and psychoses. Of particular concern to mental health professionals who have studied the effects of solitary confinement is how inmates react to conditions of reduced stimulation or sensory deprivation. Unfortunately, little empirical research exists about the effects of cell isolation in the context of supermax prisons, and the research that does exist is limited in scope. In addition, the existing research greatly varies based on the duration of isolation being studied. This makes comparisons to the indeterminacy of length of stay in supermax prisons problematic.

It may be important to examine the research that has been conducted on the psychological functioning or adaptation for inmate populations in general. Correctional psychologists, for example, have overwhelmingly indicated that depression among inmates is the most frequent clinical problem treated in prison (Boothby and Clements, 2000). This finding is not surprising considering that many studies have cited the high prevalence of depression and depressive dis-

orders among inmates (Reitzel and Harju, 2000; Toch and Adams, 1989; Zamble and Porporino, 1990). However, it suggests that many of the inmates who are eventually classified into a supermax environment may arrive with some level of depression—albeit most likely not at such a severe degree that easily can be discerned.

Also relevant to the effects of supermax confinement are studies that have been conducted on the psychological effects of length of stay and custody level. Consistent findings have emerged about the coping and adapting to prison of long-term offenders. For instance, researchers have found that inmates experience a reduction in dysphoria over time compared to the high levels discovered at the beginning of a prison term (Zamble and Porporino 1988; Toch and Adams,1989). The beginning of incarceration induces considerable psychological discomfort that, over time, leads to a slow and gradual improvement due to the constancy of the prison environment (Zamble, 1992). Researchers also have found, however, that adjusting to prison is more difficult for inmates who have less support and fewer activities and opportunities for social interaction and stimuli (Toch, 1977; Wooldredge, 1999; Wright, 1993)—characteristics that typically define supermax facilities.

Research has further shown that, excluding other variables, the level of custody assigned to an inmate is not associated with depressive severity (Zamble and Porporino, 1988). Reitzel and Harju (2000) also found no differences in depression scores for inmates classified to three levels of custody. They argue that individuals with a high external locus of control orientation (that is, belief of having little control over their lives) are more prone to higher levels of depression after a period of adjustment to prison. The researchers contend that the assessment of the personal characteristics which predispose an inmate to develop depressive symptoms—rather than type of custody and security placement—is critical to facilitating prison adjustment. Based on these findings, more jurisdictions are beginning to assess inmates to identify and flag those most vulnerable to serious mental illness prior to making any determination about a supermax placement.

Some jurisdictions, such as Ohio, do not permit the placement of inmates assessed as having serious mental illness into their high maximum-security institution, despite the on-site availability of mental health professionals. In fact, no inmate is assigned to the Ohio State Penitentiary unless he or she has been screened and evaluated for mental illness and has been found to be not seriously mentally ill.

This effort is an attempt to ensure that inmates with lifetime severe mental illness and others vulnerable to serious mental health problems are exempted from supermax confinement. Yet, despite the immense progression of assessment today, inmates continue to be inadvertently placed into the highest security levels. In other instances, security concerns may often appear to override mental health status. For example, Hodgins and Cote (1991) found that 31 percent of the inmates housed in Quebec's maximum-security Long-Term Segregation Unit suffered from a lifetime of severe mental disorder. This finding suggests that their security placement did not take mental health status into consideration.

Due to the nature of the type of inmates confined to a supermax prison, the use of cell isolation becomes a principal security measure. A range of programs and services are generally offered to inmates, but most are delivered at the inmates' cells. This practice eliminates any security risks associated with escorted moves. Arguments over inmate responses to sensory deprivation have emerged because of the highly restrictive environment and limited available movement. Grassian and Friedman (1986) maintain that studies have shown that greater degrees of deprivation under longer duration produce common responses in nonpsychotic individuals, including: a loss of perceptual constancy, perceptual illusions, hyper-reactivity to external stimuli, and the emergence of vivid fantasies. In contrast, others have found inmates confined to isolation show no decrease on visual and auditory tests and no reports of gross perceptual distortions (such as hallucinations) upon immediately leaving confinement (Gendreau, Horton, Hooper, Freedman, Wilde, and Scott, 1968; Zinger, Wichmann, and Andrews, 2001). Still others have argued that the conditions of solitary confinement are not necessarily harmful and under certain situations beneficial (Suedfeld, 1980)—thus debunking some of the arguments associated with sensory deprivation.

Unfortunately, there are wide variations in the length of time in solitary confinement being studied as well as criticisms about research methodology and sample selection (for example, sample bias: inmate volunteers, college students). Therefore, not much is really known about the effects of solitary confinement on inmate mental health. Because of the lack of clarity in the literature, what does appear to have begun is that jurisdictions are taking much more of a conservative approach toward the placement of inmates in a supermax setting based on mental health recommendations.

Security Reduction

Inmates classified into a supermax environment usually remain in that status for an indefinite period of time. Although inmates in this status are periodically evaluated for reclassification purposes, decisions on security reductions are usually based on the professional judgment of staff, which involves a determination as to whether the inmates no longer represent a high level of threat to security. In order to progress out of supermax confinement, inmates generally must move through a graduated system of levels (Ohio) or housing units (ADX Florence) based on institutional conduct and adherence to individual program and behavior plans. Due in part to the individualized program and behavior planning provided to inmates, Hershberger (1998) contends that supermax facilities are an improvement on the conditions existing in traditional segregation units because he believes that they provide more contact with staff and more opportunities for program participation.

During the assessment stage at the Ohio State Penitentiary, inmates receive orientation, and a program and behavior plan is developed for them. In Ohio, each inmate transferred to its high maximum-security institution receives an individual plan that specifies an inmate's problem behaviors and desired behavior and lists the consequences or sanctions that an inmate will receive for problem behaviors. In addition, a multidisciplinary team, known as the Inmate Program and Behavior Team (IPBT), provides an inmate with a list of required and recommended program participation to be completed. The Inmate Program and Behavior Team takes into account any prior programming the inmate has undertaken at another prison. The Inmate Program and Behavior Team consists of the institution's unit management administrator, recovery services supervisor, school administrator, mental health professional, and the inmate's appropriate unit manager. Each individualized program and behavior plan is completed within the first month of confinement at the Ohio State Penitentiary.

Inmates then must progress through four levels. Inmates begin their confinement at Level II and can either progress or regress to and from each level based on their behavior. Inmates must remain at Level II status for twelve months or longer, be in compliance with their program and behavior plan, and remain free of any conduct reports. Level I is a regression level only for inmates who have committed institutional rule infractions. Although Level I involves an indefinite timeframe, inmates are reviewed every thirty days to determine either continuance or progression back to Level II. Level III is also for an indefinite period where inmates are at the highest privilege level for high maximum security. Inmates at this level are expected to maintain the standard of conduct and pro-

gramming that brought about their placement. Finally, Level IV is for inmates who have been fully approved for security reduction and transfer from high maximum status. Level IV also has an indefinite timeframe.

As expected, privileges such as commissary, published materials, and recreation are based on the level at which the inmate resides. A "carrot and stick" approach (not unique to the supermax setting) to controlling and modifying inmate behavior continues to be used with the intent being to have inmates earn a reduction in security status. Theoretically, the use of this type of approach has an underlying inference of deterrence similar to that found in the application of incapacitation as a form of punishment.

III. Deterrence

For the incarcerated population, the threat and use of conduct reports is a primary means of formal social control in prisons (Lovell and Jemelka, 1996). Due to a positive correlation existing between rules infractions and security classification, inmates are clearly aware that major violations can and often do result in an upgrade in their security status. Perhaps more importantly, the sanctions imposed for findings of guilt on rule infractions serve as both a specific and general deterrent for future misconduct. They may be specific deterrence for the inmate who committed the infraction or general deterrence for other potential inmate violators. Either way, the fear of sanctions is viewed as a motivating force to prevent further misconduct. It therefore seems logical to assume that the presence of a supermax facility is a preventative tool for correctional administrators and a deterrent for inmates.

The concept of social control is typically examined in the context of the community, but it clearly has relevance to the correctional setting. Social control in any context involves the process of influencing the behavior of others toward conformity (Warren, 1978). At a prison level, it is easy to discern the numerous mechanisms available to encourage inmate compliance with the rules of the institution. Restrictions related to visits, commissary, and recreation and temporary confinement to segregation are only a few of the mechanisms available to promote conformity. For the consistently disruptive and predatory inmates, their behavior usually results in repeated sanctions to segregation and upgrades to higher security levels. Eventually, obtaining social control may involve placing these inmates in supermax confinement out of necessity.

A supermax prison serves as a deterrent to violent and seriously disruptive behavior throughout a prison system, which helps staff maintain order, safety, and security. Because deterrence is an intangible effect, it is important to understand its application and relevance to supermax prisons and how it relates to institutional management and operational security. First, attempting to prevent serious misconduct from occurring within the prison setting is of critical importance to effective management and security. The implications associated with volatile inmate behavior are clear and far-reaching. For instance, violent behavior by individual offenders in many instances has been the impetus to riotous acts by others. Second, the "carrot and stick" approach to managing inmates provides ample incentive toward conformity, thus enhancing the effectiveness of an institution's security measures. Third, removing inmates from the general population who exhibit behavior that jeopardizes the safety and security of inmates and staff sends a clear message: that consequences to actions do exist and will be used. Finally, knowing that their current situation can be worse—that is, by being placed in a supermax setting—can influence the decision of an inmate weighing the pros and cons associated with committing a violent offense.

No empirical studies have been identified that attempt to measure the deterrent effects of a supermax prison on inmate institutional misconduct. One could hypothesize, however, that inmate misbehavior at high-security institutions would dissipate during the initial phase of a supermax prison's operation (due to the system's need to fill beds). Also, given the indeterminate length of confinement at a supermax prison and the finite number of beds available, seeing the deterrent effect decrease over time also seems plausible.

Discussion

The reasons correctional systems find a need to operate a special management housing unit or supermax facility for inmates identified as the most unmanageable—or "worst of the worst"—varies across jurisdictions. If prison administrators were asked the question "Why supermax?" three of the most frequent responses would include management, security, and deterrence. More detailed and specific issues clearly underlie each of these three broad domains, but none perhaps most exemplify the principal reasons for the operation of a supermax facility. Although there will continue to be debate as to what constitutes the threshold of inmate behavior deserving of supermax placement, even opponents would acknowledge that a small number of inmates relative to a system's population are not, nor ever will be, amenable to traditional measures of social control. To this end, many jurisdictions have moved toward a concentration or consolidation approach to housing those inmates posing the most serious risk to safety and security. This approach appears to be the next logical step to management of the increasingly diverse and complex inmate populations.

Interestingly enough, the concepts discussed in this chapter also would have relevance to any segregation unit in existence today regardless of whether a supermax label was attached. Yet, due to the type of security measures needed within a supermax environment—most notably the housing of inmates in solitary confinement for an indefinite period—practitioners find themselves attempting to justify the existence of a supermax, rather than arguing the necessity of segregation in general. In fact, administrators often find themselves in a no-win situation. First, criticisms are forthright if an inmate is not placed in a supermax setting and shortly thereafter commits a violent or predatory offense. Second, due to the potential effects of cell isolation and other various restrictions on an inmate's mental health, criticisms occur when an offender is transferred to a supermax facility despite his volatile behavior.

It is perhaps too early in the history of supermax prisons to draw any conclusion as to whether supermax prisons will prove of be the best use of sound professional judgment and in the best interest of our society. If any direction is needed in the correctional literature, it is clearly in this area. Due to the controversies surrounding supermax facilities, drawing generalizations and analogies from past studies markedly different from the present day supermax environment is no longer plausible. Supermax prisons are unique unto themselves. Research is important for the future management and operation of supermax prisons; it can shed new light into an area that has profound consequences to departments of correction and society at large.

With public sentiment continuing to promote a tough-on-crime mindset, corrections will remain a primary focus of state and federal legislatures. However, as the field of corrections is forced to become more fiscally accountable for the increasing costs of incarceration, the spotlight will continue to focus on the need for supermax prisons.

REFERENCES

Boothby, J. and C. Clements. 2000. National Survey of Correctional Psychologists. *Criminal Justice and Behavior.* 27: 716-732.

Camp, C. and G. Camp. 2000. *The Corrections Yearbook, 2000: Adult Corrections.* Middletown, Connecticut: Criminal Justice Institute.

Gendreau, P., J. Horton, D. Hooper, N. Freedman, G. Wilde, and G. Scott. 1968. Perceptual Deprivation and Perceptual Skills: Some Methodological Considerations. *Perceptual and Motor Skills.* 27: 57-58.

Grassian, S. 1983. Psychopathological Effects of Solitary Confinement. *American Journal of Psychiatry.* 140: 1450-1454.

Grassian, S. and N. Friedman. 1986. Effects of Sensory Deprivation in Psychiatric Seclusion and Solitary Confinement. *International Journal of Law and Psychiatry.* 8: 49-65.

Hershberger, G. 1998. To the Max. *Corrections Today.* American Correctional Association. 59(1).

Hodgins, S. and G. Cote. 1991. The Mental Health of Penitentiary Inmates in Isolation. *Canadian Journal of Criminology.* April: 175-182.

Hult, K. and C. Walcott. 1990. *Governing Public Organizations: Politics, Structures, and Institutional Design.* Pacific Grove, California: Brooks/Cole Publishing.

Human Rights Watch. April, 1999. *Red Onion State Prison: Super-Maximum Security Confinement in Virginia.* New York: Human Rights Watch.

Langworthy, R. and L. Travis. 1999. *Policing in America: A Balance of Forces, Second Edition.* New York: MacMillan.

Lovell, D. and R. Jemelka. 1996. When Inmates Misbehave: The Costs of Discipline. *The Prison Journal.* 76: 165-179.

Reitzel, L. and B. Harju. 2000. Influence of Locus of Control and Custody Level on Intake and Prison-Adjustment Depression. *Criminal Justice and Behavior.* 27: 625-644.

Riveland, C. January, 1999. *Supermax Prisons: Overview and General Considerations.* Washington, D.C.: U.S. Department of Justice, National Institute of Corrections.

Robbins, S. 1990. *Organization Theory: Structure, Design, and Applications, Third Edition.* Englewood Cliffs, New Jersey: Prentice Hall.

Stone, C. 1989. *Regime Politics: Governing Atlanta, 1946-1988.* St. Lawrence, Kansas: University Press of Kansas.

Suedfeld, P. 1980. *Restricted Environmental Stimulation: Research and Clinical Applications*. New York: Wiley.

Suedfeld, P. C. Ramirez, J. Deaton, and G. Baker-Brown. 1982. Reactions and Attributes of Prisoners in Solitary Confinement. *Criminal Justice and Behavior*. 9: 303-340.

Thigpen, M. January, 1999. *Supermax Prisons: Overview and General Considerations. Foreword*. Washington, D.C.: U.S. Department of Justice, National Institute of Corrections.

Toch, H. 1977. *Living in Prison: The Ecology of Survival*. New York: Free Press.

—. 2001. The Future of Supermax Confinement. *The Prison Journal*. 81: 3.

Toch, H. and K. Adams. 1989. *Coping: Maladaptation in Prisons*. New Brunswick, New Jersey: Transaction Books.

Warren, R. 1978. *Community in America, Third Edition*. Chicago: Rand McNally.

Wilkinson, R. and T. Stickrath. 1997. After the Storm: Anatomy of a Riot's Aftermath. *Corrections Management Quarterly*. Winter, 1.

Wooldredge, J. 1999. Inmate Experiences and Psychological Well-Being. *Criminal Justice and Behavior*. 26: 235-250.

Wright, K. 1993. Prison Environment and Behavioral Outcomes. *Journal of Offender Rehabilitation*. 20: 93-113.

Zamble, E. 1992. Behavior and Adaptation in Long-Term Prison Inmates: Descriptive Longitudinal Results. *Criminal Justice and Behavior*. 19: 409-425.

Zamble, E. and F. Porporino. 1988. *Coping, Behavior, and Adaptation in Prison Inmates*. New York: Springer-Verlag.

—. 1990. Coping, Imprisonment, and Rehabilitation: Some Data and Their Implications. *Criminal Justice and Behavior*. 17: 53-70.

Zinger, I. and C. Wichmann. March, 1999. *The Psychological Effects of 60 Days in Administrative Segregation*. Research Branch of the Correctional Service of Canada.

Chapter 2: Building a High-Security Prison

Nolin Renfrow
Director of Facilities Management
Colorado Department of Corrections
Colorado Springs, Colorado

The success or failure of a high-security facility rests on three primary factors: the people, the programs, and the plant. All these factors are interrelated and must be present for an effective operation. If any of these factors are not adequately represented, the outcome can be catastrophic. If the physical plant is unsuited for the mission of a high-security prison, the people and the programs suffer. The planning and construction of the physical plant is done with the end product in mind. In this chapter, we will focus on the plant, or the building, and related systems that support the people and the programs.

If you could design your car or home, what changes or improvements would you make? How would you personalize your car? Are you as happy with your home today as the day you purchased it? If you are like most people, you always find ways of improving or modifying your personal property. What about the facility where you currently work? Are there items you would change if you had the opportunity to do so? If you have had the opportunity to tour facilities in other jurisdictions, you have undoubtedly seen buildings and systems that are worthy of emulation. And, you have probably seen the opposite—buildings that were not well planned and/or constructed.

Many of today's new prison designs are simply the physical manifestation of a warden's or director's philosophy on corrections. Often, wardens or executive staff are assigned the duty of working with design professionals to program and design correctional facilities. Some bring a wealth of knowledge and experience to the table, and some do not. More often than not, placing one person "on point" for design development results in a less than satisfactory outcome (*see* Witke, 2000).

The best approach to programming and designing a high-custody facility is to involve the various disciplines that will eventually work in the facility. An eclectic gathering of subject matter experts broadens the experience base and brings many new ideas and concepts to the process. Group planning also allows people in one discipline to see how their decisions will affect other disciplines. Hopefully, the final product is one that has been developed through consensus and represents an understanding of the interdependence of functional areas within the facility.

Where Do We Begin?

Before a facility can be designed and constructed, there must be a demonstrated need for the facility. In the corrections business, the need is generally justified through either trend analysis or actual conditions. Trend analysis is a forward-looking process that identifies future needs and has time built in to ensure that the facility is delivered when it is needed. Trend analysis is difficult in the corrections field. Many uncontrollable variables can affect population projections such as changes in sentencing laws or governmental leaders, or court decisions affecting release procedures. Dealing with changing variables means the planning process needs to be flexible and responsive to changing circumstances.

Need demonstrated through actual conditions is how many jurisdictions receive funding for a new facility. Having an immediate need is not a good position to be in, because the time period between the funding and occupancy of a new facility can take years. If you have an immediate need, conditions will only get worse since you do not have lead-time built into the process. If a prison is needed today, it will probably be overflowing by the time it is built. In the meantime, existing prisons must deal with the crowding and associated issues.

Because most jurisdictions have a controlling authority, the request must be submitted for review and approval by that authority. In some instances, it may be the state legislature or county commissioners. Regardless of the structure or nature of the controlling authority, the same things are needed to make a decision on your request:

- accurate cost estimates
- design and construction timetables
- evidence that you have looked at less costly alternatives

With many requests, you may need to present a long-term planning scenario or master plan. It should show how this facility fits with existing facilities and how it will play a role in future requests.

Often, achieving funding for a high-security prison is difficult for political reasons. Be aware of, and sensitive to, the concerns of the citizens and their elected officials. Not all citizens and elected officials are convinced that high-security prisons are either cost effective or conducive to prisoner reform. For these reasons, those advocating for a new facility must emphasize the program aspects of the new facility. Contemporary programs in high-security prisons must deal with:

- inmate idleness
- sensory deprivation
- mental health needs
- rehabilitative efforts
- a tiered system of progression that is tied to inmate behavior and program participation

The day of locking inmates up and throwing away the key is long gone. Many high-security prisons across the nation have had tremendous results with a programs-oriented model. Using the experiences and data collected from these facilities will go a long way toward alleviating the concerns of citizens and government officials.

Determining the Cost of a High-security Prison

For the sake of discussion, assume that you have accurately determined the size for your future facility to be 1,000 beds. How much money do you need to request? The easiest, least costly, and most erroneous way to determine the projected cost is to simply multiply the 1,000 beds by an average cost from another jurisdiction. For example, suppose the national average cost per bed for a high-security facility averages $120,000, and you simply multiply that cost by 1,000 beds. You would conclude that you need $120 million to build your new facility. Getting to that figure was certainly easy. Determining the average national cost per bed probably did not cost you anything, but your estimate may be way off. But remember this point: whatever money you are funded to build the facility is what you will have to live with. One hundred twenty million dollars may be adequate in Arkansas but extremely short in Alaska.

So, what are the factors or variables that contribute to the variance in per-bed costs? First, the site or location of the facility can significantly affect the cost of construction and operation of any prison, not just high-security prisons. Prison sites in rural locations can have a significant site location premium if there are not enough skilled workers in the area. Contractors know they are going to have to pay premium wages to attract construction workers to remote locations—especially if the construction market is booming. Aside from the geographic location, the specific site itself can significantly affect costs. For this reason, a site and infrastructure analysis must be conducted to compare the comparative impact of various proposed sites. Most site and infrastructure analyses evaluate the following:

- soil conditions
- site access
- site grading issues
- proximity to public utilities
- environmental concerns such as toxic waste or endangered species
- initial cost of the site
- public support or opposition
- site location premiums compared to baseline costs for other proposed locations.

In a large-scale project, the potential for variation between sites can be millions of dollars. Additionally, sites must be examined for the labor pool needed to run a high-security prison. Remember, high-security prisons need a large cadre of mental health and medical staff. These professionals can be hard to find in rural or remote locations.

Aside from site costs, what other types of conditions can affect the cost of building the facility? The construction market at the time of bidding the job will play a big role in determining the final costs. If the construction market is booming, and you are bidding in this market, be prepared to pay a premium. When all the contractors are busy, they are hesitant to take on more work; some may be beyond their bonding capacity. Their bids will reflect what they believe is the added risk of stretching themselves out too thin. Another contributor to higher costs in a boom period is labor. If workers are in short supply due to a lot of construction activity, they can require and get a higher wage. Quite simply, it is the law of supply and demand.

Another construction-related issue that can affect the cost of a new prison is a shortage of one or more critical components needed to construct your facility. More than once, there has been a nationwide shortage of cement. Shortages of a material will result in higher prices and possibly affect the schedule. Currently, there are only a handful of manufacturers and suppliers of detention-grade security equipment (that is, doors, windows, and controls). The final cost of these components, and timely delivery, may depend on the size of your facility and the relationship you have with the manufacturers and suppliers.

The list of items that will affect the cost of constructing your facility is almost endless. The list provided above is just a sampling of variables that must be considered when putting together an estimate for your capital construction request. The services of professional estimators and design professionals are essential in formulating the accuracy needed to secure adequate funding. Often, the best approach to obtaining proper funding is to request "study" money in one fiscal cycle. Then, you can come back later with the formal request based on the results of your study. At a minimum, "study" money should include:

- an infrastructure and site analysis
- some level of programming (we will discuss programming later in this chapter)
- an estimate to construct the facility and an estimate of the annual operating cost

What Comes after the Funding?

The most important step in designing a correctional facility actually occurs before the formal design process begins. Many people refer to this critical planning component as "programming." Programming is to design as planning is to a trip to Mars. Simply stated, a trip to Mars is nothing more than building a huge rocket, aiming it at the big red planet, putting some people and food on board, and lighting the fuse. As ridiculous as this sounds, some people take the same approach to designing a prison. The author has encountered many people who do not want or need any help designing a prison. After all, they have worked in prisons for years. Another simplistic approach is to "just build me one like the one I visited in Escapeville."

Corrections is an evolving science and art. The prisons of today look little like the prisons of a generation ago. The people who work in our prisons are unlike their predecessors, both in skill and knowledge. Contemporary correctional systems are always looking for better ways of doing business. One of the primary reasons our prisons are so much better than they were a few years ago is because of the programming process. The same can be said about many things, such as automobiles, electronics, appliances, and communications systems. Better design stems from, and is dependent on, programming.

A few years ago, this author had a supervisor who wanted the work group to: "Identify all the things we haven't thought of, and get me a list so that we won't be blindsided when one of these things occurs." This request is one of the most idiotic, or brilliant, ever heard. There is some brilliance hidden in the request. It infers or implies the importance of identifying problems before they occur and having systems or people in place to handle them.

Programming aims at identifying current and future problems, and eliminating them before they occur. Programming also goes one step beyond problem identification; it asks the basic question, "How can we do things better?" To answer that question, you need to involve the most innovative and experienced staff in the programming sessions. Automobiles become better not by designers unilaterally deciding what the public wants but by asking the public what it wants and designing it.

Similarly, design professionals should not merely design a facility for you but rather design it based on the information that you, the owner and operator, provide. For this reason, selecting the proper design team is imperative for the success of your project. Many potential design firms will give you a list of all the correctional facilities "designed" by their firm, hoping you will be impressed by their collective experience. Frankly, some of the best design firms the author has encountered have never designed a correctional facility. This is not to say firms that have experience are not well suited for your project; it just means that the best firms are the ones that rely heavily on you—the owner and operator—to interpret your input into a fully functioning design that will serve your needs for many years.

Selecting a Design Team

After you obtain funding, a design team will be the first team to come on board. "Design team" is a term used to describe the architects, engineers, and specialty design firms and consultants that are responsible for producing the final construction documents. The team is part of a traditional design/bid/build approach. With this approach, the facility is entirely designed by the design team, put out for bid to the construction contractors, and built to the specifications outlined in the contract documents. Under other delivery strategies—such as design/build or construction management—the selected contractor is also present during the programming and design to offer his or her expertise in cost estimating and constructability reviews. We will learn more about delivery strategies later in this chapter.

Do not be surprised if design professionals contact your agency prior to your project being funded. They review trade journals and communications systems to identify upcoming jobs. Because you operate in the public sector, your projects will be highly visible, and early on they will express interest. Properly executed, the contracting person or division of your agency will advertise the project and release an RFQ or RFP (request for qualifications or request for proposal) to the public in general. The RFQ will give a brief description of your project, the scope of work, and possibly the amount of money available for the project. The contracting person will invite design teams to submit a document (or packet) that is geared toward convincing your agency that they are the best suited (or qualified) to perform the design work for this project. The submittal process usually involves a review of all the proposals by a group within your agency. If there are numerous submittals, you may decide to narrow, or short list, the field to the five or six firms that appear well qualified to perform for you. At this point, you may decide to directly interview the short-listed design teams and ask further questions or to let them put their best foot forward. When you have finalized the interviews, you are then challenged with selecting the best-suited firm.

Prior to the interviews, you must develop a scoring mechanism that is applied equally to all the applicants. Factors can be weighted, but they must be objective in case the selection is contested or appealed. It is perfectly all right, and preferred, to ask the prospective designers to list all of the talent they bring to the project. Talent includes those individuals within their particular firm and outside engineers and consultants. You may want to interview all of the proposed design team members prior to making a final selection. Last, but not least, ask for each team's level of commitment to keeping the people listed on their submittal on the team for the duration of the project. Do not fall for the old bait and switch.

Once the design team has been selected and a contract executed, the predesign activities can begin. It is good to begin by having the design team challenge, or at least revisit, the assumptions made about the project. For example, if you put together a "needs assessment" in your request for funding, you might want to revisit that assessment with the design team. The best design teams are those that ask questions including questions based on information presented by the owner. Take the design team on a tour of some of your existing facilities. Make sure that they are familiar with where you have been so that they can assist you in setting the team goals on where you want to go.

Speaking of goals, establish them early and with the assistance of the design team. We all want the world's best correctional facility, or the most progressive programs in the nation, or a model for all other jurisdictions. But boiling these down into meaningful goals and objectives is time well spent. While you want the world's best correctional facility, the guy in the mailroom just wants more space. The goals and objectives of all of the programs within the facility must be fully articulated and challenged.

Good programming sessions occur when the facilitator keeps asking "how and why." If the physical plant manager wants to have a very efficient operation with dependable equipment and systems, ask him or her how it is intended to be done. If the answer is "need more space," ask why. If the manager needs more space to store attic stock, ask why. If the manager says the current space is too small, ask why. If the manager says it is too small because ten years ago part of the space was given to vocational programs, ask why. If the manager says the space was not needed ten years ago but is needed today, ask why. The purpose of "how and why" questioning is not to irritate or aggravate the participants. It is to get a sense of their needs, their ability to communicate their needs, and their ability to defend their needs.

One of the purposes of programming is to understand each subprogram's space and adjacency needs. Space drives the cost of the facility; adjacency is an efficiency concern.

Adjacency addresses the programming questions of "how do goods, people, and services move through the facility or site?" To answer these questions, you need to know something about the mission of the facility and the operations that will be carried out there. Because we are focusing on high-security facilities, we need to understand the operational activities of the facility; how they occur, where they occur, when they occur, why they occur, who does what, and so forth. The conceptual design cannot begin until all of these details get ferreted out.

Conceptual design is much different than actual design. Conceptual design is often called the "napkin sketch." Because you undoubtedly will do many conceptual designs, the process is often called "scenario development." An example of this process is to draw "bubble diagrams" on a chalkboard. The first bubble might be the kitchen represented by a large circle. Remember, at this stage you have not designed the kitchen, much less its size. For this exercise, the size is unimportant.

Someone may ask the question, "Where does the kitchen need to be located within the facility, or does it even need to be located within the facility?" This simple question will immediately spark a heated debate. The food service manager might say it does not need to be inside the perimeter because the food will be served in the units. The manager envisions a carting system that takes the food to the unit, either bulk or pre-served and distributed there. In fact, the manager prefers being outside the perimeter because receiving warehouse shipments will be easier. Given this information, the facilitator places the food service bubble or circle outside an imaginary perimeter.

The security or custody supervisor strongly objects to placement outside the facility because it means inmate workers will have to be escorted to the kitchen—or, worse yet, be brought in from another facility. To the security supervisor, this arrangement drives the need for escort staff and opens avenues for contraband through the food service process. The warehouse manager will proba-

bly support the food service manager to avoid losing time delivering commodities inside a secure perimeter.

The job of the facilitator is to let the discussion continue as long as it appears to be either informational or moving toward consensus. If the discussion continues for a long period of time and is not headed toward resolution, the facilitator will either table the discussion and move on to another area, or call on the lead facility representative to make a decision.

Often, the lead facility representative will be the warden, or equivalent, who will eventually run the facility. Therefore, the warden has the ability to make people happy or upset even before the facility is operating. Hopefully, the lead facility representative will be highly experienced and have the goals and mission of the future facility in mind when making decisions during the predesign process.

Scenario development can take days, weeks, or months, depending on the size and complexity of the facility and the quality of the programming team that is leading the process. If you can only take one pearl of wisdom from this paragraph, let it be this: it costs virtually nothing to make changes during programming; it costs a little to change them during design; and it costs tremendously to change them during construction. For this reason, programming can be the most cost-effective and best time spent on the whole project. To take it one step further, decisions made during programming will affect the operations of the facility for the life of the facility. Therefore, make well-reasoned decisions.

Are There Other Predesign Activities?

The work product of the predesign process is a document known as an "operational program plan." This document, generally a text document, details the activities of every subprogram in the facility. Remember the discussion in programming about "how do goods, people, and services move throughout the facility and site?" The operational program plan is the document that details:

- how this happens within each subprogram
- its relationship to other subprograms
- the staffing needed to perform these functions
- the hours of operations
- equipment needed to operate efficiently
- the space requirements of each subprogram
- adjacency requirements to other subprograms

From this document, an overall staffing plan for the facility starts to evolve along with the identification of positions and posts. The operational program plan is important for many reasons. First, it gives the owner/operator a document to review that is reflective of all the information gathered in programming sessions. Secondly, it gives the architect and design team an understanding of the owner's needs and serves as a starting point for the actual design of the facility.

After the operational program plan is fully developed and approved, the next activity is developing the architectural program plan. The architectural program plan is a document that is usually text but may include some sketches that the architects, engineers, and consultants develop as a response to the operational program plan. In other words, the design team is starting to put the information gathered in programming sessions and the architectural program plan into a format that makes sense for design purposes. Spaces are now beginning to become more fully defined; adjacency relationships are being fully developed; scenarios are being reduced to the few that make the most sense; and the facility layout and site requirements are being more clearly defined.

If properly and thoughtfully completed, the architectural program plan will give the owner the first accurate glimpse of the site and facility layout, preliminary cost estimates, preliminary construction durations, and budget breakdown. Once both program plans have been approved, the design team can begin the actual design work.

What Are the Stages of Design?

After the operational and architectural program plan is developed, the design team begins the actual design process. Designing is a linear process, with three main stages. The first stage is "schematic design" or SD. Schematic design is a conceptual design that is the design team's first attempt to characterize the information gathered from programming into an actual facility layout. You can expect to see floor plans that are presented in drawings with proper scale. Although a schematic design may not contain a lot of detail, it is adequate for the owner/operator to get a sense of the size of the facility. There should also be an estimate of construction costs for the facility. Because the design is very elementary at the schematic design stage, the design team will usually give themselves a fairly wide margin of error when estimating the cost of the facility.

In other words, be prepared for a fairly high-cost estimate and hints that the original scope of work needs to be revisited or that "value engineering" will need to occur. Value engineering is a process in which you look at the systems included in the buildings and site to see if alternate, acceptable systems can be substituted in an effort to save money. Value engineering is different than scope reduction. Scope reduction is the actual elimination of buildings or square footage to reach the target budget.

The second stage of design is known as "design development" or DD. Design development is a more refined level of design where actual costs of construction can be estimated more accurately. The specifications begin to be developed at this stage and include the following:

- The types and quality of materials to be used are listed.
- The methods of acceptable construction are defined.
- The minimum quality standards are set.
- Actual performance data for equipment and systems are listed.

Cost estimates are more easily projected at this more complete level of design. The design team may actually "shop" the design development drawings to the construction trades for estimates. Having the construction trades provide estimates gives the design team more accurate information on the cost and schedule. It is important to remember that the design team is usually obligated by the contract to design the facility to meet the owner's budget. If you receive an estimate at the design development level that far exceeds the available funds, the design team is primarily responsible—due to negligence during either the programming stage or at the schematic design stage. If at the design development level the indications are that the facility cannot be built for the budgeted amount, expect the architect to call for either more value engineering, scope reduction, or both.

If it appears the project can meet budget, then the design team proceeds to the final design stage, that of "contract documents" or CDs. Contract documents are the final set of drawings and specifications that are put out to bid. They are highly refined and, if properly developed, give prospective contractors all the information they need to bid on the job. Poorly prepared contract documents lead to problems during construction. If the documents are not clear when bid, they need revision. Revisions during the construction period are very costly and directly affect the construction budget. Remember, the further along in the process the revisions occur, the more costly they are. Changing the location of a room during schematic design may cost nothing, but changing it after the contact documents stage is extremely costly.

The time frames for planning and designing a supermax vary based on several factors:

- the size of the facility
- the experience of the design team
- the experience of the owners/operators
- how much new technology is being used in the new facility

Generally speaking, the design processes take about one year.

Construction Delivery Strategies

One of the decisions the owner needs to make during the design process is what construction delivery strategy makes the best sense for the project. Sometimes, the architect or design team assists with this decision. Construction delivery strategy is a term that outlines the relationships among the owner, the architect, and the contractor, and how they can be optimized for all parties. The easiest way to visualize the construction process is to imagine it as a triad relationship among the three individuals. At each corner of the triangle is one of the participants. Each party brings resources to the project and exposure or risk. The contractor, for example, brings many resources to the job and carries the risk of his or her costs exceeding the contracted price of construction. The architect brings resources and has risk in not designing the project within available funds or has potential liability for designing faulty or inadequate buildings. The owner brings the monetary resources to the project but risks spending them on poor quality work and possibly having schedule problems.

These examples provide only a few of the resources and risks each participant experiences on every project. Because each project is different, the best delivery strategy for each project may be different. For example, earlier in the chapter we discussed a very traditional delivery strategy known as design/bid/build. It is a very linear process, and each party's role is clear. The architect wants to design a quality facility, have the bid come in under the available funds, and see that the contractor meets all the requirements outlined in the drawings and specifications.

Contractors want to have all of their subcontractors perform in an efficient and cost-effective manner, manage the job effectively to minimize unforeseen costs, and meet the schedule to protect the firm's reputation. The owner wants the budget and schedule met, and to have a final product that will perform up to expectations. This process all seems like a tight package that is easily accomplished. If everyone performs as expected, then there will not be any problems.

In reality, there are plenty of problems with this strategy. If there were not, there would not be other strategies to choose. Other delivery strategies exist simply because the traditional design/bid/build strategy is often fraught with problems. The primary problem is that every party tends to look out for his or her own best interests. If you are a savvy owner, you can hold your own in this process. But what if you very seldom engage in the construction process? What if you do not know how to protect your interests?

If you as an owner want an advocate in your corner, you can use a different strategy such as construction management (CM) or program management (PM). In this process, you pay a fee for a knowledgeable ally to assist you in the process. In some variations, the construction manager or program manager will also act as the general contractor and manage the various trades. The supposed advantage in this strategy is that the construction manager or program manager is more aligned with the owner than the subcontractors. But, like the traditional design/bid/build process, there can be serious difficulties arising from this strategy.

A third approach is design/build. This process is basically an alliance between the construction contractor and the designers to share information, expedite the construction process, and give the owner a final product that is the result of the combined wisdom and experience of the designers and builders. But, this process has pitfalls as well.

If a design/build team is not adequately experienced in the design and construction of prison facilities, the work product will reflect the inadequacies of the team. Additionally, if the owner is not technically sophisticated, the ability to monitor the project from conception to completion is severely affected; the result may be reduced quality and reliability of the final product. Finally, in a design/build environment, the owner assumes a much larger role in ensuring adherence to the specifications set forth in the construction documents. The owner must either have construction-related professionals on staff or contract for additional inspection services to monitor the progress and quality being delivered by the design/build team.

There are many more delivery strategies from which to choose. Several books and articles have been written on the advantages and disadvantages of each. An important thing to remember about delivery strategies is this: any strategy will work if all the participants are competent and trustworthy; the opposite is true as well. One of the best ways to ensure the quality of the participants for your project is to establish minimum selection criteria that will prequalify designers and contractors. Incompetent designers and contractors should not be allowed to compete for your work. If you have questions about prequalification criteria for your jurisdiction, you may want to consult your procurement department or become familiar with statutes and regulations that govern public procurement.

Information Specifically for High-security Facilities

The information provided thus far can apply to any correctional facility. But what about high-security facilities, or "supermax" facilities? What should be done differently or additionally when building a high-security facility? When we consider the design and construction of these facilities, one thing must be understood. A failure of the buildings or any of their related security systems will have devastating results, including loss of life, loss of property, and compromised public safety. Failure by staff also can have devastating results. The good news is that there are new and emerging technologies that will compensate for staff error. The bad news is that you can never rely heavily on new technology as the primary security system in a high-security facility.

The best security is a combination of highly trained, motivated staff and security systems and equipment that form a complete and integrated security system. Aside from visible architecture, security systems should be invisible to the inmate population. Managers should take special effort to control security information developed during programming and design. This action will minimize the chances of inmates having access to the invisible operating systems behind the security devices. Wherever they go, inmates should see cameras and monitors. However, inmates should not see the electronic systems that manage these devices.

Lethal fences are a tremendous psychological deterrent to an attack on the perimeter. Do not make the mistake of allowing inmates access to the design documents that may reveal the system design. Make sure that background checks are done on anyone associated with the project, including design team members, contractors, subcontractors, and laborers. Account for and inventory every set of drawings and specifications issued by the architect. Restrict access to this information to the people on your staff who need to know it to perform their duties.

One should not undertake designing a high-security facility without the assistance of a qualified, nationally recognized security consultant. The consultant can either contract directly with your agency or through the architect. Most jurisdictions seldom build high-security facilities. If more than a year or two has lapsed since your last high-security project, use the services of a consultant. Security consultants should be aware of all the technologies and systems available. They also should know the reliability and service record of systems that are in place in other jurisdictions. Security consultants also keep up on the technology transfer information that is being accumulated in various agencies across the country. Do not make the mistake of assuming that your security manager can design the security systems because she or he has thirty years of corrections experience. Designing today's highly complex, integrated security systems requires a complete understanding of:

- electronics
- security hardware
- computer design and configuration
- perimeter detection products
- communications backbones and devices
- fiber optics
- data storage
- standby and emergency power generation, and so forth

Consider your thirty-year security veteran an adjunct to the security-design process.

Because the inmates in a high-security facility are a high risk to the general public, staff, and other inmates, the ultimate design configuration needs to reflect security concerns. In most jurisdictions, inmates housed in supermax facilities spend up to twenty-three hours per day in their cells. Thus, cells become one of the primary inmate containment items in the facility. They are constructed typically of high-strength and highly reinforced concrete, grouted and reinforced masonry, or steel. The furnishings within the cells are permanently attached to the walls or floor by equally strong attachment devices. If inmates can remove a piece of cell furniture, they can use it as a demolition tool and/or use it to fashion weapons.

Each cell is situated in a larger security envelope, usually called a dayhall or pod. The dayhall will house a number of additional cells, usually about sixteen to twenty. Secure separations between dayhalls isolate inmates and minimize the chances of a small-scale disruption spreading throughout the facility. Dayhalls are usually enclosed within larger units, sometimes referred to as special housing units. This arrangement provides another envelope of security. These units are generally part of a larger security envelope, possibly a wing or section of the facility. Many supermax facilities have six or seven security envelopes from each cell to the outside of the facility. The exterior perimeter of the facility is usually the last, and often most secure security envelope between the inmates and the public. This "layered" approach to security presents an extremely daunting challenge to escape.

In the typical configuration of the cell house, the cell fronts are perpendicular to the control center/observation area that controls the doors and monitors inmate movement. Typically, the control center is the center of a hub of dayhalls. This arrangement generally requires more than one control operator due to the number of dayhalls that need to be visually monitored. Another design detail is that the dayhalls are two rows of cells high, certainly not more than three. Keeping the height of the top tier relatively low reduces the chance of severe injury or death should an inmate or staff member fall off the tier.

The actual operation of the supermax constitutes a security component. Almost all services and goods are delivered to the inmates in their cells. This operating practice severely limits the inmates' access to areas outside their cells. When outside their cells, the inmates are usually full restrained and escorted by at least two staff members.

Because most, if not all, services are delivered to the cells, adjacencies are very important. Food is delivered three times a day, and delivery can be complicated and lengthy. Therefore, food service should be placed in a location that is central to all the high-security living units. Many jurisdictions place medical examination rooms and barber rooms either in the living unit or immediately adjacent so that inmates do not have to be escorted long distances for these services.

One of the most important adjacencies is the placement of offices for unit supervisors and managers in relationship to the unit they supervise. Given the constant operational demands associated with operating a supermax unit, supervisors should be "officed"

immediately adjacent to their units—preferably in an area that has direct observation of the activities within the unit.

Site lines are extremely important in a supermax environment. When designing a supermax, the teams should try to envision how goods, services, and people will move throughout the facility. When these paths are defined, you must insist that direct site lines are needed in situations where inmates will be moving; where staff is working in inmate occupied areas; and where inmates will spend time out of their cells, such as recreation. In the rare circumstance where direct observation is not possible, such as on stairways, cameras should be strategically placed. The best designs are those that minimize the use of cameras and monitors to see an area. Sometimes, cameras are placed in areas that also have direct visual observation such as dayhalls so that activities can be monitored and recorded.

The construction materials for a supermax are generally limited to concrete, steel, and reinforced masonry. All locks and security hardware should be commensurate with the level of construction, whether locally or remotely operated. This practice holds true for at least the first three or four security envelopes (that is, the cell, the dayhall, the living unit, and wing or building). The same holds true for corridors, offices, and examination rooms that inmates will access by escort. Outside the most secure envelopes and in administrative office space, the construction materials can change to less expensive building systems such as stud walls, commercial grade locks, and moveable furnishings and equipment.

Special attention should be given to the security systems, particularly those operated electronically. Most supermax facilities rely on sophisticated low-voltage security control systems to aid in the operation and surveillance of the facility. During design, a high priority should be placed on direct, unobstructed observation of inmates and staff. In areas where direct observation is not possible, cameras and monitors are essential. Staff and inmates should never be in a place where they cannot be observed either directly or on monitors. Cameras and monitors are a great deterrent to inmate misbehavior. Inmates are less likely to act out when they know they are being observed, and the activity is probably recorded. Most of today's electronic security systems also feature data logging (every event and status is recorded on tape or disc). Passive detection systems such as infrared or movement detectors can set off an alarm when people are in areas that should not be accessed. Detection systems associated with the external perimeter of the facility are essential.

The inspections that occur during the construction of the facility are primarily needed to ensure compliance with the construction documents. Inspections should primarily focus on the security-related components of the facility. An example would be to examine all of the ductwork that penetrates security zones to ensure that specified grill work is in place to keep inmates from moving throughout the facility in the duct work. Another example would be to watch the masonry installation to ensure that the reinforcement bars and required grouting are added per the specifications. There is a big difference in the strength/security of a standard masonry wall and one that is properly reinforced with rebar and mortar. Another security inspection is to test every field device, whether it is a door, camera, intercom, or life safety device to ensure that it functions as detailed in the design documents.

Inspections also should address the quality and workmanship of the contractor. Contractors generally perform differently if the owner or owner's representative exposes them to regular inspections. Most contractors welcome these inspections because they provide feedback as to the acceptability of the work product.

Last but Not Least

Most of this chapter has dealt with the physical aspects of a high-security prison.

From experience, this author can state that the most critical components of a successful high-security facility are the programs and the people. The key to inmate management, regardless of custody, is reducing idleness and involving inmates in programs aimed at moving them back into general population facilities. Ten years ago, high-security facilities were warehousing inmates. The program was simple: lock them up for twenty-three hours a day, and let them recreate and shower the other hour. The new program is as follows: lock them up twenty-three hours a day, let them recreate and shower the other hour, but provide quality interaction and in-cell programming. Interaction with custody staff and program staff is critical to the success of high-security operations. Teachers and program staff can provide educational, mental health, substance abuse, anger management, and other programs via closed-circuit television with visits at the cell door.

The final, and most critical, component is to provide the inmates a recipe for working their way out of high-security confinement. Devise a tiered incentive system that systematically progresses inmates out of the facility and back into the general population. The program should be meaningful and not just a series of hurdles that the inmate must jump through to progress. Do not make accumulating more personal property a component of the program. Inmates in high-security prisons should have only the bare essentials for hygiene and their studies. Positive incentives for behavior can be things such as increased time on the phones, better visiting hours, movement to showers, exercise without an escort, and so forth.

Be sure to include the staff members who work with the inmates in regular status reviews. If the staff knows their input is considered when evaluating the status of an inmate in the program, they will take their job much more seriously. They will begin to work with the inmates to assist them through the system. When inmates realize the front line staff members are key in determining how inmates progress, their behavior will change dramatically. And isn't that what our business is all about?

REFERENCES

Witke, L., ed. 2000. *Planning and Design Guide for Secure Adult and Juvenile Correctional Facilities*. Lanham, Maryland: American Correctional Association.

Chapter 3: Developing the Mission and Goals

James D. Hart
Associate Warden
Dodge Correctional Institution
Waupun, Wisconsin

Introduction

For the management of any agency or organization, it is crucial that each employee knows:

- the purpose of the agency or organization
- what the agency or organization is attempting to accomplish
- the means by which it seeks to accomplish its goals

This chapter will explain what a mission statement is and how the staff can strive to work together to achieve the goals of the agency or organization.

A mission statement is an organizational statement of purpose. It sets forth the reasons for the existence of the facility and, generally, its contextual relationship with the rest of the system. A mission statement will reflect the fundamental core values of the agency and will do so in a way that shows its uniqueness. A good mission statement also will serve as a touchstone for staff in performing their responsibilities. That is, it will be the reference point when questions may arise as to the ethics or behaviors within the facility. It will serve as the guiding principles of the institution. Three examples of agency mission statements are as follows:

1. Federal Bureau of Prisons: "It is the mission of the Federal Bureau of Prisons to protect society by confining offenders in the controlled environments of prisons and community-based facilities that are safe, humane, cost-efficient, and appropriately secure, and that provide work and other self-improvement opportunities to assist offenders in becoming law-abiding citizens."

2. Colorado Department of Corrections: "The mission of the Colorado Department of Corrections is to protect the public through effective management of offenders in controlled environments which are efficient, safe, humane, and appropriately secure, while also providing meaningful work and self-improvement opportunities to assist offenders with community reintegration."

3. Wisconsin Department of Corrections: "The Department of Corrections will protect the public through the constructive management of offenders placed in its charge. The mission will be accomplished in the following ways:

- providing levels of supervision and control consistent with the risk posed by the offender

- assuring that staff and offenders are safe
- assuring that staff function professionally, honestly and with integrity
- being responsive and sensitive to victims, victims' families and a diverse community
- providing for the humane and respectful treatment of offenders
- providing opportunities for the development of constructive offenders' skills and the modification of thought processes related to criminal behavior and victimization
- treating a diverse workforce as valued partners by fostering staff development and effectiveness
- providing and managing resources to promote successful offender integration within the community.
- holding offenders accountable for their actions through sanctions, restitution, and restoration
- developing individualized correctional strategies based on the uniqueness of each offender.
- Being accountable to taxpayers through efficient, effective and innovative management of resources.
- actively responding to staff victimization and promoting wellness.
- educating the public on what we do and how we do it."

A mission statement for a supermax facility identifies basically who is doing what to whom, for what purpose, and how it is to be done. It is the statement that sets the direction and the purpose of the facility and gives meaning to the daily activities of the staff. As a unique facility in a system, the mission statement for a supermax facility highlights this uniqueness and describes its specialized function for the system as a whole. It will reflect, in a global sense, the institutional philosophy in dealing with inmates in its custody. The mission statement is typically a brief and concise statement that directs the operation of the facility.

Two examples of mission statements for a supermax facility are as follows:

1) "The Wisconsin Secure Program Facility, Wisconsin's most secure facility, safely and humanely houses, manages and controls inmates who demonstrate serious behavioral problems in other settings. WSPF provides inmates the opportunity to acquire skills needed for their possible integration into less secure correctional environments."

2) Colorado State Penitentiary's high-security management: "Our Mission is:

- To preserve order in all Department of Corrections facilities by effectively managing dangerous/disruptive offenders in a safe, secure and humane environment
- To change offender conduct through incentive based behavior modification and cognitive programs which facilitate offender reintegration into less secure environments
- To promote a culture which mentors and encourages staff professionalism, career enhancement, positive morale, and pride."

The goals are the statements by which the staff of the facility will strive to meet the intent of the mission. These goals are specific in terms of guiding staff behavior in regards to the mission. In this respect, the goals are more behaviorally oriented than the mission statement, which is philosophically oriented. Individual goals should relate to staff interactions with inmates, with other staff, with facility management, with the community, and with other identified entities.

These goals will also reflect the facility's vision and values as it seeks to conduct its business of managing and modifying the high-risk population in its care and custody. Goals are very significant in setting forth institutional expectations for staff who will be dealing with a particularly dangerous and risky inmate population. Two examples of goals of the Colorado State Penitentiary include developing an inmate evacuation plan and developing a lesson plan on forced cell supervision.

The Mission

Typically, the mission statement for a supermax facility is dictated, in large part, by its specialized function in a larger system, in other words, the removal, housing, and treatment of high-risk inmates. The function is a piece of the larger correctional system and, as such, the function must be articulated in the mission statement. This practice serves to identify and justify specialized treatment and different modes of operation from other facilities within that system. These differences are made explicit, as are the reasons for these differences in the mission statement.

The mission statement needs to be a written document. Its intent needs to be clear, and its dissemination needs to be wide. Many constituencies have an interest in corrections in general, and with incarceration, specifically. As supermax takes incarceration to a higher level, interest becomes heightened.

- Corrections professionals are interested in the effectiveness of isolating and modifying a disruptive and assaultive population.
- Courts become interested because of litigation about conditions of confinement initiated by inmates in supermax facilities.
- Politicians become interested because of budget requests as they relate to staffing and resource requests for these unique facilities—and complaints from inmates and their families.
- Inmate advocacy groups become interested because of philosophical objections to the nature of supermax confinement.
- The media is interested because of the high profile of supermax facilities.

A written, widely disseminated mission statement gives a basis from which to begin interactions with these constituencies. This document will provide a clear statement by which these constituencies can understand (though not necessarily agree with) the purpose of the facility. It also becomes the document by which the facility can be held accountable by the public. As a publicly funded institution, the facility must be open to review of its operation and performance. The public measuring stick is its success in accomplishing the mission set forth for the facility.

The supermax facility is a part of a larger system and its purpose supplements other elements of that system. Therefore, much of the mission of the supermax is already established by the legislation authorizing its existence and by its architectural design. These pieces lay the legal and physical foundations. But the philosophical principles of the facility are the responsibility of the warden and those the warden invites into the process of the mission development. Key administrative staff should be included to ensure their input relative to their areas of responsibility within the facility.

Consulting with and/or visiting administrators of other supermax facilities to the extent possible is also advisable. The more one can benefit from the wisdom and experience of others who have had similar responsibilities, the more one is able to avoid pitfalls or mistakes, and maximize the positives of others' experience.

Establishing a community board composed of representative interests from the surrounding area can serve to widen the base of both input into and support for the mission statement—and the operation of the supermax facility. This practice invites the participation of outside representation in formalizing the mission and, through the formulation process, generates broader support for the ultimate product. The practice also ensures broader dissemination of and education about the mission statement. Representatives are able to speak for the facility and represent its function as they move through their respective circles.

Once established, the warden and leadership team need to clearly understand the mission and articulate this mission to other staff in the facility. This group needs to periodically review and discuss the mission to ensure its prominence as a guide for the facility and to maintain focus on the mission. The warden clearly has lead responsibility for the process and must demonstrate leadership and commitment to the ideals set forth in the mission statement.

The warden and facility administration need to ensure continuing awareness of the mission on the part of staff and inmates. This task can be done in a number of ways. First, posting copies of the mission statement in prominent and public areas guarantees its availability. As management staff move through the facility, they must engage staff and inmates in discussions relative to the philosophy and the mission of the facility. Management staff should both correct and compliment staff members' job performance and conditions within the facility; these comments should relate to the mission.

As new employees join the staff, they must be oriented to the facility's mission. They should be provided with a copy of the mission statement in their orientation material. In addition, they should attend orientation sessions designed to introduce them to the leadership team. This practice gives the leadership team an opportunity to:

- review the mission statement with new staff
- demonstrate their endorsement of it
- discuss and clarify its meaning
- institutionally address the concepts reflected by the mission
- articulate their expectations to the new staff

Supervisory staff must continue to focus on and emphasize the mission on a regular basis. This task is accomplished through regular "rounds" of responsibility areas, through regular staff meetings, and through employee performance evaluations. Each of these techniques can be used to engage staff in discussions about the facility and its mission, to assess staff understanding, to provide clarity, to correct misperceptions, and to reinforce appropriate understanding and behavior.

Ensuring that inmates understand the mission of the facility in which they are housed is also important. This goal becomes even more significant in a supermax facility where the ultimate goal is to assist the inmates toward reintegration into the general population at another facility. Agreement with the mission is not necessary, but knowledge and understanding of the mission is. Such knowledge lets the inmates know (in a general sense) why they are at the facility, what the expectations are, and how they can appropriately interact with their environment. The staff, in turn, can then reinforce the mission as they work with the inmates.

On a continuing and ongoing basis, the management staff must be proactive in reinforcing the mission throughout the facility, to the community, and to external constituencies. This means holding staff accountable for acting appropriately and professionally at all times as well as engaging in corrective actions and discipline, as necessary. It means ensuring that staff receive proper training in dealing with a high-risk population, and it means maintaining appropriate supervision of staff and inmates by management.

It also means clearly setting forth expectations for inmate conduct and holding inmates accountable for their behavior. The prompt, fair, and consistent administration of a disciplinary system in compliance with the facility mission will clarify and reinforce expectations for both inmates and staff. The system is a mechanism that can provide either positive or negative reinforcement for inmate behavior—depending on the pattern or progress which the inmates display through their behavior.

Because every facility is located somewhere, establishing a relationship with that "somewhere" is significant. There will be financial relationships with local businesses, inmate visitors in the area, and a number of staff members living in the vicinity. Therefore, it is important to ensure that the local community understands the mission of the facility and is provided with timely and accurate information about the facility. The facility management should be proactive in providing information to the community; should aggressively respond to false or misinformation about the facility; and should seek ways to contribute to the local community both through staff and inmate efforts. There should be interdependence in terms of mutual aid agreements.

The facility mission should be reviewed periodically by the warden, the community board, and the management team to ensure that it continues to reflect the intent of the facility. As social and political elements and expectations change, the mission of the facility may need to be refined and revised to reflect these changes. Or, internal conditions may dictate revision of the mission statement. Changes in the larger agency also may require review and modification of the facility mission. Staff should be continually encouraged to review and propose refinements to or modifications of the facility mission statement. As the warden and management team adopt changes or refinements, these again must be clearly articulated and communicated to the various constituencies. The team then must establish the expectation that such changes will be fully incorporated into the facility and its operation.

Goals

Once the general purpose of the facility has been defined, the next task is to provide guidance and direction to staff in fulfilling this purpose. The warden and the management team accomplish this task by identifying the goals. These goals establish the facility's expectations on how staff at all levels will go about the business of the facility. The facility goals are targets, not boundaries—that is, they are what is to be achieved as opposed to the limits of acceptable behavior. Therefore, goal statements are developed in affirmative language that prescribes conduct rather than in negative language which proscribes conduct.

Good goals have many benefits:

- Unify staff by operationalizing the facility mission in terms of expectations for staff behavior. In this respect, staff are striving together to accomplish the same thing. Being unified should enhance levels of cooperation among staff because they are able to see how interrelationships with others enhance their own performance.
- Provide standards against which performance can be measured. This situation applies to both individual employees and the facility as a whole.
- Provide information to the public about the functioning of the facility and, therefore, enhance the public's understanding.
- Enable the facility to assess itself in terms of accomplishing its mission.

Goals must be realistic and achievable in terms of the facility's resources, staff's expectations, and targeted end results. Goals also should be prioritized. Achieving everything the facility wants to accomplish may not be possible. In fact, some goals may occasionally appear to conflict, for example, treatment versus security. Therefore, the management team must ensure that staff know which goals take precedence.

Tracking progress toward achieving goals can be a simple process. Management staff can walk through the facility and talk with various staff and inmates. This practice serves two purposes. First, management staff can assess informally the staff's and inmates' perceptions and understanding about the goals. Second, management staff can measure informally staff's and inmates' perceptions about achieving goals through feedback.

Goals also can be tracked and evaluated formally through shift or climate reports and logs. These reports will reflect a tone or tenor of the facility which, in turn, will reflect progress toward or regression from established goals. For example, the goal "provide a safe and secure environment" can be demonstrated by shift reports documenting the absence of problematic behavior. Goals also can be reviewed and discussed at management team meetings and at departmental meetings. Finally, the facility may track the progress of achieving goals by conducting a self-review or audit, which may be managed by internal or external parties. The facility should periodically review its goals both in terms of achievement and of the mission and redefine them as necessary.

Establishing expectations through goals involves layers of responsibility. This means that some goals may be more specifically relevant to one segment of the facility than another. For instance, a goal relating to the safe, secure, humane treatment of all inmates in the facility is most specifically relevant to the management team. The goal compels the management team to enact correctional practices that will address this goal. Other staff have a responsibility to act in accordance with this goal but they do not have a similar capacity as the management team to accomplish this on a facilitywide basis.

Likewise, a goal such as holding inmates accountable to the rules is more relevant to the day-to-day functioning of line staff. The management team clearly has an interest in the achievement of this goal. But line staff have more capacity to ensure its achievement than the management staff who will have less frequent and direct interaction with the inmates housed in the facility.

Despite the difference, all staff have responsibility to maximize the facility's ability to achieve its goals. Because they guide and direct staff behavior in a consistent fashion, goals serve a unifying function for all staff. Goals also serve to remind all staff that they are "on the same side" and that they are responsible to the mission of the facility.

As the mission statement is defined by the uniqueness of the supermax facility, so too are the goals that address the responsibilities of dealing with the facility's high-risk population. The management team will set the tone for the facility through the development and implementation of the goals it defines for the facility. As these goals are developed and articulated, ensuring that they are disseminated and understood throughout the facility is once again critical.

Supervisory staff throughout the facility are responsible for the implementation and achievement of facility goals in their areas of responsibility. Each supervisor must ensure that his or her employees are aware of the goals of the facility. This task is accomplished through regular staff meetings where both the mission statement and goals are reviewed and discussed and during employee evaluations.

The evaluation process enables the supervisor to translate facility goals into individual performance objectives for each employee. These performance objectives should be clear, measurable behavioral statements that further the goals of both the supervisor's area of responsibility and the goals of the facility. The process clearly gives each employee behavioral expectations and measures against which job performance will be evaluated during the review period. Through the process, each employee has the opportunity to clarify expectations through individual discussions with the supervisor and to receive feedback in terms of meeting the facility's goals. The process also provides each employee with a mechanism to share input into or to suggest refinements to or revisions of the facility's goals or mission statement. Such information will be "sent" upward through the chain of command.

Inmates also need to be aware of the goals of the facility. Each inmate is entitled to know how to earn a transfer to the general population. Each inmate should be made aware of the goals (target behaviors and timeframes) to be achieved for being moved to a less restrictive environment. For those motivated to change or to leave, the goals will identify what the inmates need to do; for those not so motivated, the goals will tell the inmates why they stay.

In making assessments as to who leaves and who stays, having a multidisciplinary approach and input is critical. Ensuring that each discipline recognizes its own area of expertise and the expertise of other disciplines is also critical. Everything that occurs in a facility is a piece of the facility program. Each piece feeds the other pieces. When all staff and all operations intermesh, the facility will be more successful with more inmate behavioral change. Good security and good programs do not conflict. They are each an integral part of the program. A good program encompasses programs and security. One cannot be successful without the other. In this regard, positive professional tension existing between disciplines (such as security and counseling) is useful. Such professional tension raises staff awareness of not only its own function but also the function of other disciplines. The staff of each discipline learns to maximize its own function, while simultaneously recognizing and respecting the legitimacy and function of other disciplines.

However, reaching this point requires a high degree of cooperation and professional respect, which can be fostered by establishing performance expectations that require mutuality and teamwork to achieve the facility's goals. For example, security staff has a clear and overriding interest in maximizing security in any correctional facility. Case management staff also has a clear interest in security. But they also have professional interest in and responsibility for providing access to appropriate programming to mitigate problematic behavior on the part of inmates. Once inmates complete appropriate programming, the case manager should make this fact known. The manager then should advocate for the inmates being placed in a situation where they can demonstrate the achievement of appropriate skills. This situation may require advocating for increased privileges for the inmates or transfers to less restrictive settings—requests that may be contrary to recommendations of the security staff. Professional responsibilities and performance expectations require the manager to access whatever review mechanism is in place in that jurisdiction.

Likewise, medical staff may recommend or prescribe treatments, medications, physical aids, or other items with which security staff may take exception. As these circumstances occur, line staff directly involved with the inmates must bring their conflicting interests to the attention of their respective supervisors. These supervisors, in turn, can bring the issues to the facility management team for accommodation or resolution. Often, circumstances will occur in which legitimate medical requirements may need to be accommodated by enhanced or modified security procedures. Staff should learn to view these occasions as opportunities for them to work together toward accomplishing their goals and achieving the mission of the facility—rather than as power struggles between different segments of the facility.

When they assess inmates, staff of psychiatric services may also find themselves at odds with security staff. The isolation and restriction of a supermax setting dictates more frequent psychological monitoring and potential recommendations for security checks, medications, or transfers for psychological or psychiatric reasons. These recommendations may not be compatible with perceptions of line security staff. In these instances, all staff should document their observations and professional recommendations and forward these up the chain of command for consideration by those responsible for making the ultimate decision.

Security staff should be willing to ask for intervention techniques. If every employee in the facility responds to the inmate in a consistent manner, inmate behavioral change will occur more quickly. The question is how to do the job more efficiently, not who does the best job.

When all the disciplines work together, they become more effective than the sum of the disciplines working individually. This situation can be achieved with training, multidisciplinary goal setting, and problem resolution. Security and mental health staff should view each other as supporting one another.

All levels of staff need to recognize and accept the fact that doing their job is more difficult, time-consuming, and cumbersome because of the nature of the supermax facility. It is a facility that is necessarily governed by a very high degree of security because of the clients which it houses, and high-security procedures are not convenient. This situation poses particular challenges for areas such as facility maintenance staff. They may require security staff escorts to perform their duties, frequent tool and material inventories, and more staff labor instead of inmate labor than found in a more traditional institution. On a superficial or routine basis, such requirements appear to complicate job responsibilities or make it harder to do the job. But staff must understand that attention to these enhanced procedures simply makes the facility a safer place for all staff in it.

Staff acceptance of a multidisciplinary approach is enhanced by a clear understanding of the decision-making process within the facility. That is, staff members need to know to what extent they can make decisions versus the extent to which they can make recommendations. The management team of the facility must explicitly delegate and identify decision-making authority through its formal chain of command. The team also must model the notion of "positive tension" between and among disciplines within the facility. This situation, again, requires professional respect on the part of the management team and an affirmative demonstration of teamwork from those representing different areas of responsibility. Apparent problems of irreconcilable divergence are better viewed as opportunities for the management team to demonstrate and model goals of cooperation, respect, and mutuality of interest in achieving the mission.

Summary

An agency or organization does not exist in a vacuum. It has a purpose and a context. To be successful, the agency must develop, articulate, and disseminate its purpose. It does so through its mission statement. To be successful, the agency must ensure that its staff is aware of the mission and the goals by which staff, individually, can contribute to achieving the mission. Both the mission and goals need to be clear and to be understood by management, by line staff, by the inmates in the facility, and by various interested constituencies. Agreement or consensus on the mission or the goals is not necessary. But having all parties clearly understand the fundamental purpose of the facility and the means by which this fundamental purpose is to be achieved is necessary.

Chapter 4: Staffing a Supermax Prison

James M. Greco
The Greco Group, LLC
Canon City, Colorado

Introduction

During the often-challenging process of requesting funds for the construction of a supermax correctional facility, much discussion centers on staffing. Characteristically, the civil service sector tends to spend the largest percentage of its budgets on employee pay and benefits. Therefore, carefully analyzing the facility's program and mission in all areas of the internal operation is important.

Carefully developing a justifiable staffing template is essential in selling the facility's concept that will have the scrutiny of legislative decision makers and also the media and the general public. Undoubtedly, these stakeholders will need to be educated about the purpose of such a prison, including providing explanations about staff duties and responsibilities. Stereotypical images that promote myths about cruel, untrained staff who treat inmates inhumanely in a dark, austere, warehouse environment will need to receive a quick and appropriate response.

Moreover, planners must know that staff/offender ratios or formulas used in the past are not likely to be applicable when defining position and post requirements in a supermax prison. Until the function of the facility's daily program is fully understood, inaccurate assumptions about the number of staff needed to operate this facility may lead to a tendency to underfund the operation. As experienced correctional professionals know, however, the higher the offender-custody level being managed, the greater number of staff needed to perform the daily work. Never is that more true than in the supermax environment. Whatever the task is—food service, laundry, mailroom activity, or providing educational and recreational programs—it probably will take longer to accomplish and require additional staff and the necessity of finding creative solutions to challenging operational dilemmas.

Not only is the quantity of staff an important consideration, the quality of staff selected to assume the varied and important job assignments is just as important. The success of any workplace environment hinges on the loyalty and dedication of employees who share a vested interest in its purpose. Correctional workers assume a grave responsibility for the offenders they manage. The success or failure of all internal functions of a supermax facility usually can be related to staff members' ability, at all ranks and levels, to do the following:

- follow policy
- make decisions
- solve problems, with consistency, from one shift to the next

There is a tendency to blame a variety of facility performance deficiencies on the types of offenders being housed in the supermax facility. But the professional demeanor and level of staff capability will be the greatest link to the prison's successful operation. The supermax prison environment was once thought to be a radical approach to housing the "worst of the worst." It has evolved, however, into a concept where difficult-to-manage offenders can, in fact, be managed humanely and with attention to meaningful use of offender time. Staff and their professional approach to custody and care are the primary reason for the program's success.

Workplace Culture

Fostering the culture of the supermax workplace begins with a tone communicated from the top down, starting with approval from legislative decision makers. Expectations about the facility's ability to protect the public and to understand the types of inmates housed there are best established in the early days of program design. The vision, mission, values, goals, and objectives of such a facility should be tied to other components of the agency.

Consideration for the part such a facility plays in the agency's overall operation will keep staff aware that they are not working in an isolated vacuum. Instead, they are a part of the agency's larger plan for inmate supervision. The overall mission and goals and objectives should be developed as part of a structured strategic plan that can be used as an instrument for regular monitoring, tracking, and reporting.

Standards, which include principles related to service, accountability, commitment, competence, and partnerships, are best established early, reinforced regularly, and used as a foundation for staff training. When this philosophy includes the affirmation of staff contributions, the often-difficult days of the early stages of facility activation will be more tolerable—especially given the level of staff stress, usually inherent in the supermax environment.

Once the supermax warden and management team have been selected, establishing operational policy and procedure is certainly critical. However, a shared understanding about the working atmosphere desired in such a facility is equally important in a number of areas. First, agreement about the emphasis and time to be placed on developing, supporting, and empowering professional correctional staff to manage high-risk, dangerous offenders is essential. Second, consensus from the headquarters' executive staff down about building the supermax team through intensive training and mentoring is also essential. Third, a thorough understanding of the nature of offenders being housed—their propensity for violent behavior, escape risk factors, gang affiliation, and so forth—will lead to successful daily management and supervision. Finally, important discussions and well-communicated philosophy around zero tolerance for the following are necessary:

- demonstration of a "door warrior" mentality. A "door warrior" is an aggressive staff member who acts unprofessionally by lashing out at an individual who is locked up and cannot attack the officer. The situation is similar to taunting a dog who is chained. This behavior causes problems because the inmate may become resentful and lash out against the next staff member who walks by the cell. Officers who exhibit such behavior must be reprimanded.
- inappropriate use of force
- violation of the staff code of conduct
- enforcement of their (staff's) own interpretation of "punishment"

The warden and management team likely will be looked upon favorably by both inmates and staff when team members are visible in housing units, interact throughout the facility's various departments, and model appropriate behavior and problem solving. This practice, commonly known in correctional settings as "management by walking around," provides opportunities to discuss issues of importance and provides immediate feedback—which is essential when defining and creating the workplace culture.

Staff Selection

The search, screen, and selection process of staff assigned to a supermax setting is relative to the desired level of success for all components of the program. Due to the unique nature of the facility, some staff with specialized credentials are required to provide specially designed programs and services to offenders. But the day-to-day business is accomplished through the efforts of line staff in housing units, food service workers, maintenance staff, and so forth. Important security requirements may call for staff to work together in pairs or larger groups in a variety of situations:

- internally moving inmates within the facility
- accompanying medical staff in housing units during dispensing of medications
- facilitating intake and orientation of new offenders to the facility
- performing on specialized teams during planned use-of-force incidents
- responding with specific tasks during real or simulated emergencies

However, encouraging a cross-disciplinary approach to communication with other kinds of supermax staff—such as teachers, librarians, case managers, recreation specialists, treatment providers, chaplains, and so forth—will go a long way toward ensuring accuracy of exchanged information; protecting against staff manipulation by inmates; breeding esprit de corps; helping develop a shared vision; and generally creating a safer workplace.

Staff discover that they likely will have to perform nontraditional duties to meet institutional needs. In addition, staff may be called on to assist others in work areas unfamiliar to them to maintain the good order of the facility. Staff should expect this situation and prepare for it.

Two schools of thought exist about supermax staffing. First, some experts believe that only seasoned, experienced staff should be considered for such work. They can be held to a higher professional standard, and thus the learning curve, basic correctional training and safety risk factors, are more easily managed than by bringing a totally new staff on board.

The disadvantage to this practice is that these experienced staff may be predisposed to carry negative biases into the supermax work environment. Security staff may openly judge inmates housed in the facility. In addition, such staff may believe that the inmates—due to the nature of their criminal history—do not "deserve" to have unusual efforts made on their behalf for programs or treatment in a one-on-one fashion. Worse, some seasoned staff will articulate their personal opinions and biases directly to these offenders and engage in a sarcastic war of words. With a locked cell door between themselves and the inmates, even experienced staff have a false sense of security and may, under stress, communicate a heightened sense of bravado.

As it becomes clearer that supermax inmates are unable to do much for themselves and are totally dependent on services provided by staff, resentment grows. The resentment is often intensified by the inmates themselves who try to push the reaction buttons of supermax staff. Such behavior often results in the escalation of a full-fledged incident which, when analyzed later, could have been prevented, had the staff members not personalized the interchange. This "door warrior" behavior may have a deleterious effect on professional staff, as they could become the scapegoats for inmates' retaliation.

Seasoned correctional employees are often shocked and irritated to learn that the daily supermax routine includes frequent cell door contact with inmates, whose every need—such as delivery of mail, meals, or toilet articles—is provided by correctional line staff. The remainder of the shift is spent in writing reports; reconciling safety and security equipment inventories; moving inmates to places such as the visitation area or clinical services; completing janitorial cleaning tasks; or reviewing post orders, policies, and so forth. This revelation is in sharp contrast to how the experienced staff members viewed their role prior to being assigned to this unusual setting.

Hiring new, inexperienced line staff enables the administration to immerse these staff into the desired philosophical culture and convey an understanding of the facility's mission. This process is usually readily accepted, without the color or influence of personal bias. Operating on the theory that these staff "don't know anything different" produces a potential workforce that adapts to change easily and enthusiastically. However, supervisors who hire inexperienced staff also should be aware of the learning curve between training and practice. Lack of experience, poor judgment, and the inability to make effective discretionary decisions often snowballs into a series of pitfalls, which can be both dangerous and costly. There is a greater risk of new hires making amateur mistakes during the execution of routine tasks, which, if not corrected quickly, could lead to unsafe security practices. New staff may not be intimately knowledgeable about policy, fail to use the chain of command appropriately, be easily manipulated by inmates, or react too quickly without evaluating the situation from all angles. New staff have a tendency to become involved in excessive use-of-force incidents or, conversely, fail to respond at all when needed.

Ideally, a healthy mix of both new and experienced staff should be considered, if possible, when staffing such an environment. In fact, agencies should communicate with their human resource divisions well in advance of job offers being conveyed, to ensure that recruiters have correct information about the nature of the facility's program. Effective recruiting strategies should be used early to provide accurate information to prospective job candidates and dispel rumors. This practice is especially important for agencies which have had little experience with the supermax approach to offender management. Otherwise, many preconceived notions about the "worst of the worst" inmate population and employees needed to staff such a facility will abound. Remembering this key point is important: staff breeches in procedure that lead to safety risks or other fatal flaws usually can be attributed to human error; responsibility is shared with both experienced and new staff equally.

Many correctional agencies and related personnel systems are bound by periods of probationary performance, seniority policies, union contracts, or bidding processes that will play a part in establishing the staffing patterns for supermax prisons. Overtime pay, compensatory time, or hazardous duty pay are also elements for consideration and mechanisms for promotional opportunity.

Hiring criteria and testing for working in any correctional environment is essential. Law and policy may prohibit the supermax administration from requiring more than is required for other correctional settings. However, including the following criteria during the staff selection process is important:

- basic screening
- testing and measuring assessment of potential employee literacy
- having problem-solving skills
- having the ability to interpret policy and procedure
- assuring a level of wellness/fitness
- having the ability to respond to a rules-based code of ethical conduct

Both the interviewer and the candidate will benefit from the use of frank discussions involving open-ended, scenario-based questions during the interview process. This strategy will eliminate doubt about the nature of the job and will firmly communicate the agency's expectations about working in a supermax setting; typical post assignments and future rotation; shift scheduling; and so forth. Some measure of a candidate's willingness to supervise offenders who display anti-social characteristics and exhibit violent, manipulative, or predatory behavior is also needed.

Therefore, well-structured interviews should provide the framework to identify those would-be supermax workers who are truly sincere about learning new and different skills, following directions, and conducting themselves professionally. Candidates often will reveal behavioral tendencies about themselves, which may be appropriate in other correctional settings but are generally undesirable in the supermax environment. For example, candidates may:

- value machismo; they may feel big, strong, and cocky, and express this verbally. Such behavior is in contrast to someone who is level-headed, knows the job, and does it well.
- have a past history of aggressive behavior.
- use unprofessional language such as "I kicked butt with those inmates" or "I'm the best at what I do," which is an indication the candidate probably is not appropriate for the supermax setting.

Finally, interviewers should reassure job candidates that mentoring and opportunities for coaching and assistance will be readily available to ensure their successful job performance.

When interviewing specialized staff to deliver educational programs, recreation, substance abuse treatment, religious services, and so forth, hiring authorities should evaluate candidates' eagerness to consider new and distinct methods of providing these services. For example, offenders are not permitted outside their cells to participate in traditional classroom academic education. Therefore, supermax teachers must be able to use alternative methods of program delivery, remain flexible, and work collaboratively to discover the most effective means of supplying educational materials and services—within security constraints common to the supermax environment. In fact, the same is true for all treatment providers. Meeting or exceeding the expectations of American Correctional Association standards requires

creativity with accurate recordkeeping and active support of institutional or agency policy. Specialized staff should be prepared to defend their program design from legal inquiry to prove that offenders' programmatic needs are not ignored.

A supermax facility's physical plant design and purpose will affect all of its operations. In addition to program delivery, areas such as food service and laundry should be analyzed for staff workload and efficiency of operation. Normally, a work cadre of inmates from less secure environments is used to assist staff in performing certain support functions. This means that kitchen and laundry staffs are required to practice good inmate supervision and be observant about contraband issues while providing services to inmates. For example, food service staff will have to contend with special diet requirements and transportation of meals to housing units. A smooth and functional operation is dependent on staff assigned to those areas.

Teaming a professional staff is not possible without paying attention to diversity and balance of gender, age, and ethnicity. While expectations are that the agency's policy will support this component of staffing pattern, the ability of a management team to actually recruit and retain a diverse workforce depends on many issues.

For example, not so many years ago, female staff were thought to be unable or unwilling to accomplish correctional-related work. In fact, deep prejudice and resentment against females in the profession were often openly expressed. While women were generally struggling in other workplace arenas to have their contributions validated with equal pay for equal work, correctional work environments created unique staffing challenges. First, women were eager to complete training and take their place alongside male counterparts. But the women quickly discovered that the work environment was not friendly to the notion of females being placed in positions where safety and security were tested daily. Physical plants, where restrooms and privacy had never been an issue before, suddenly were out of step with new legal requirements associated with the workplace. Uniforms generally were not tailored to fit the female form, so females everywhere patiently adapted until appropriate uniforms became standard.

Second, male corrections staff were often torn between two feelings. They were resentful of these women for breaking into a largely male-dominated culture. But the men also were obligated to not only watch their own backs but also be prepared to protect or rescue a female correctional worker who found herself in harm's way. Questions about a female correctional worker's ability—to render assistance, use force when needed, serve as a suitable partner, master vigorous training related to self-defense or firearms—became cultural barriers almost impossible to overcome. Discrimination and sexual harassment claims skyrocketed to the attention of legal systems across the country. As a result, state and federal law forced agencies to draft new policies to allow women to become integrated into a variety of corrections-related jobs. Further, swift consequences were set in motion when it could be proven that females had, indeed, been subjected to less-than-equitable treatment or respect.

Today, an increasing number of women are being socially and economically accepted into corrections-related fields, including supermax prison settings. Representation of women is common among all types of corrections jobs and at all levels of rank, including supermax female wardens. Supermax staff and inmates alike have benefited from the presence of a female workforce and more than ever, welcome their participation in housing units, on emergency response teams, and in positions of power and authority. Female correctional workers have proven that they can master the skills, execute them when necessary, and actually offer a tone and presence in a supermax setting which is beneficial for all, including the offenders.

Ethnic balance among staff is often difficult to achieve due to a workforce pool, geography, or other factors. However, when super-

max prisons demonstrate that staff represent a broad sampling of the ethnic world at large, communication, trust, teamwork, and safety are enhanced. Offender populations often take on a posture of respect and tend to communicate in nonthreatening ways when diverse staff serve in a variety of roles in the supermax setting. The management team of a supermax prison is responsible for sending a powerful message about valuing all staff and encouraging an enriched balance in an environment where teams and partnerships abound. When supermax offenders observe that demonstration of unity and support, game playing and attempts to defeat the system are not easy to accomplish.

Clearly, the supermax staff workload is different from that in other correctional settings. A number of vital facility operations are needed to adequately and smoothly meet the daily mission; staff are needed in greater numbers to perform these roles. The staff selection process, which clearly establishes work performance expectations and preference criteria, is a vital step toward achieving a successful facility program.

Volunteers

The use of volunteers in traditional correctional settings has long been a practice used to enhance staffing, especially in the areas of offender programs. Some agencies, however, choose to disallow such services in supermax settings, and use paid, full-time program staff to deliver services such as chaplaincy. Other agencies have discovered that while using volunteers is still possible in a supermax environment, limitations about the frequency and types of uses for volunteers require special consideration. Offenders are confined to their cells each day, and there is a general principle of "no contact" applied to visiting room protocol. Therefore, nontraditional approaches for using volunteers can be useful and positive, albeit creative.

With proper training and orientation, religious volunteers will play an important role in assisting management teams. Supermax institutions will benefit from recognized and approved experts who provide accurate information related to a number of allowable religious or faith practices. As a result of federal legislation applied to incarcerated persons, however, supermax wardens find themselves trying to balance security needs and practices with meeting the intent of such law. Property considerations, diet, alternatives to congregational assembly, and other challenges can be solved when agencies use religious advisors and mutually agree on sound alternatives. Further, sensory deprivation claims by supermax offenders are decreased when provisions are made for a door-to-door cell contact form of ministry. Distribution of religious print materials by such volunteers also demonstrates on the part of administrative teams that respect for religious practice is being promoted. Religious volunteers also may be encouraged to use videotapes or other closed-circuit broadcast methods to minister to prisoners throughout the institution.

In supermax housing units, one-on-one counseling or prayer in front of a cell door becomes very public. However, when institution staff are knowledgeable about the advantages of such cell-door contact to overall offender management, coupled with security oversight, they become more likely to realize that the benefits outweigh inconveniences. Normally, other offenders being housed nearby will also respect that time of cell-door contact. In short, prison fellowship activities often take on a greater importance in this setting. When appropriate, such services play a vital role for fulfilling the need to provide outside stimulus, primarily because many supermax offenders receive few visits.

Many supermax staff are confused and frustrated about the lengths to which prison administrators will require staff to go to meet the various and demanding needs of inmates practicing their faiths. Staff find it ironic that while many routine privileges associated with quality of life are lost when offenders are assigned to this setting, faith practice rights remain in place. Supermax staff are often unfamiliar with the norms of the various religious groups which emerge in a setting such as this one. They are skeptical of the offenders' sincerity about practicing such a religion. Further, these staff often resent that special considerations for scheduling, meal service, and allowable property items are necessary. In fact, staff members discover that they themselves are required to facilitate the offenders' ability to practice religion in a variety of ways. This concept may fly counter to their notion of severely restricting the activities of the supermax inmate and their notion of how the supermax setting should be defined. However, using the religious volunteers in staff training, sharing information, organizing a system of validating offender property, and becoming knowledgeable about the agency's and facility's ability to maintain security will promote partnerships rather than create a chasm where staff are on opposing sides.

It is best to take a proactive approach with this issue before being legally challenged. That is, strong agency policy, reviewed by appropriate legal advisors, should be developed, trained to, and followed by everyone working at the facility. During training, staff can be reminded that, just like with medical services, mental health treatment, or academic programs, religious volunteers advance the goal of meaningful use of time for offenders. Staff may resist and grapple with a policy that they interpret to seem to afford the "worst of the worst" with greater religious privileges than what staff themselves enjoy. However, responsible wardens and other upper management staff will recognize that they are expected to endorse such policy, lead by example, and impart a sense of professionalism where everyone is included in acceptance and preservation of the offenders' rights. Training, endorsed by a number of subject matter experts, is key to overcoming these challenges.

Most agencies use the assistance of a number of nationally recognized volunteer organizations to provide offender services beyond those solely religious in nature.

These organizations may rely on contributions or private benefactors for a financial base and have been known to provide prisoner family transportation, nursery supervision in visiting rooms, and other incidental donations. Undoubtedly, agencies will want to develop policies to govern the oversight of such organizations and judge their usefulness in a supermax setting.

Training programs for volunteer staff should include not only information about basic security and operational functions but also strategies to minimize the risk of being perpetrated by antisocial offenders. Volunteers should have the ability to communicate with full-time staff—such as institutional volunteer coordinators or sponsors—who can advise them when inmate manipulation appears to be interfering with the mission of the program and security practice. It is not unusual for some volunteers to believe that they are capable of bringing out the best character traits of the inmates. However, the harsh reality is that many of these offenders will prey upon well-intentioned volunteers in divisive and self-serving ways. In fact, dangerous behaviors demonstrated by violent inmates, sex offenders, or gang members may actually be in furtherance of criminal activity. How does this happen in a confinement setting where no physical contact is possible? The answer is that due to distorted thinking and prior experiences, sophisticated offenders often see a genuine desire by the volunteer to help as a weakness; an opportunity to exploit a perceived vulnerability; and an excellent mechanism for personal favor and gain. In calculated ways, they craft cunning forms of communication, even through a physical barrier. Over time, volunteers may take small liberties with institutional rules and become influenced or tricked to give favors to inmates. Without good institutional staff supervision, volunteers may become complacent and actually believe they are "helping" offenders. Through difficult lessons learned, many volunteers discover too late that they came to serve the institutional population for seemingly noble reasons. But

they are being dismissed from the facility and barred from entry into other facilities systemwide.

Training

Over the years, correctional agencies have vastly improved their approach to training staff for work in prison settings. In fact, most agencies today look upon all staff working in jails and prisons as correctional workers, regardless of their defined job classifications. This philosophy is in sharp contrast to the days when staff were merely issued a set of keys and instructed to report to an area of the facility—after a brief tour or welcome from the warden.

Today, government agencies recognize their responsibility to impart information to employees, which is not only useful and in keeping with state or federal law but also supportive of agency policies. Historically, the lessons learned from past prison disturbances across the nation—where control of facilities has been lost and men and women have been injured or killed—can be connected to lack of training or poor training practices. Legal battles have been won (or lost) over the quality, consistency, and extent to which staff are instructed on a variety of topics. Correctional agencies today also recognize their moral obligation to prepare staff to work in environments where being in harm's way is inherent to the work. When staff understand that everyone has been trained to respond consistently (and they appear prepared to step in to provide back up without a moment's hesitation), both staff and visitors can observe a sense of quiet confidence throughout the facility.

Effective preservice training programs, using guidelines set down by the American Correctional Association, include a variety of modules on prison work. Curricula should reflect the current national thinking, be legally defensible, and be aligned with federal law, state statutes, and agency policies. Performance-based learning objectives should be established for each course taught, with attention paid to adult learning theory. Successful completion of such preservice training programs should be based on observable and measurable outcomes. By including every job classification in this preservice program, camaraderie begins to build. This unity, when carried over into the supermax workplace, sends an important message to inmates and makes their ability to play staff against one another in divisive ways more difficult to accomplish.

Once new staff are on the job, giving them time for institutional familiarization and orientation provides them with initial exposure to the mission of a particular correctional setting. This orientation period may include additional or specialized training classes. For example, distinct teams are often used to perform specific duties relative to offender management. Emergency response, forced cell, shakedown, and disturbance control teams (and so forth) require additional use-of-force training and instruction on impact weapons, special munitions, chemical agents, canine support, and so forth.

Newly assigned supermax staff are usually anxious to become involved with the daily activities and work. They soon discover, however, the reality of an increased workload during certain key timeframes of the day and during certain shifts of the twenty-four-hour period. For example, meal delivery, recreation, health, and comfort item delivery, escorting, and so forth require intense activity during the day shift.

Staff also discover that due to the nature of the inmate population, interruptions to scheduled operations may occur at any time. Such interruptions may take the form of unplanned, disruptive events, often developing into incidents, which become staff intensive. For example, suppose the traditional meal schedule is interrupted. Because staff scheduled to distribute those meals to inmate cells are pulled away to perform other duties associated with the incident, other staff must assume that meal delivery responsibility.

Once a resolution occurs, after-action protocol will require report writing, debriefing, interviewing, and so forth. Only then can staff refocus their efforts back to their regular duties and responsibilities. When count fails to clear, or tools, keys, or other equipment items are missing, all institution staff are affected. Shifts may be required to stay over into the next working period, programs or visits may be terminated, and training may be suspended. This roller coaster effect takes its toll in contributing to staff stress, lower morale, and so forth. However, if staff are trained to prepare for these situations, negative consequences are decreased. Security problems are less likely when all staff are security minded and aware of consequences of lapses in security procedures.

During an orientation period, new or transferring employees should be schooled in the facility's philosophy of supervision. Understanding this philosophy provides the continuity for the institution balance that should exist in the supermax setting. Clear expectations about the facility's mission, level of professionalism expected, history, and tradition should be communicated to new hires. They should be asked to set aside preconceived notions about what they thought working in such an environment would entail. Instead, the orientation period should include opportunities to provide information about the program's core values, vision, and expectations for any staff member assigned to work in the supermax setting. New hires or staff transfers should be trained in day-to-day operations of other arears than their specific work area. They also should gain an understanding of all working posts/ positions, thereby leading to an eventual common understanding of how all pieces of the puzzle fit together. Having this information, especially in correctional systems where supermax prison staffing numbers are large, will foster respect and appreciation for what everyone does to support the mission on a daily basis.

Agencies may approach the integration of staff scheduling in a variety of ways. Some correctional systems prefer to assign all new staff to shifts of high institutional activity and designate a senior staff person to monitor and coach, as needed. Others prefer to schedule new staff during the lowest time periods of activity, to set aside blocks of time for reinforcing specific skills. Still other agencies will send new staff into the facility environment after successful completion of a portion of the preservice program. After an established institutional familiarization period, the staff are required to return to the training academy to complete the course of study. There are clearly advantages and disadvantages to all these methods of bringing new staff on board. Agencies should reevaluate the effectiveness of these training programs through annual staff surveys.

Staff hired from the community may have little or no background in corrections. However, administration can teach these employees properly and train them from point A to point B to point C. They start with a few weeks of general training on all aspects of the facility's operations. Then, the staff attend a training program where they meet all the other new staff and learn facility procedures. Finally, the staff come back to the facility and are assigned to their specialty and assigned mentors from experienced staff. Such staff have no bad habits. Therefore, the advantage is that they are able to be molded.

Staff who are transferred to the facility have a background in corrections. On the one hand, they may have some bad habits and may be unwilling to use supermax procedures, opting instead to "stick with their preconceived ideas." The situation is similar to teaching an old dog new tricks. On the other hand, these staff may be exemplary employees who are willing to learn different procedures for a supermax. In this case, they can be mentors for other staff. If experienced staff stay in boundaries, follow policies and procedures, help keep other staff safe because they are good communicators with inmates, then the staff will be excellent facility team mem-

bers. These staff will follow the adage, "Be firm, be fair, be consistent."

Experienced staff transferring or promoting into the supermax environment will require the same orientation period. Administrative teams should provide a means by which these staff, accustomed to offender supervision practices among less restrictive populations, can be assimilated into this restrictive environment—where internal policy influencing offender movement, property, searches, use of force, and so forth are defined in alternative ways.

Perhaps one of the most critical training areas for staff working in the supermax setting is in interpersonal communication, with emphasis on avoidance of confrontational techniques. The combative tendency of supermax inmates tends to lead to their unwillingness to comply with rules, direct orders, or even routine behavior expectations. If such behavior is not controlled, a war of wills and words between staff and inmates can escalate quickly.

Staff are expected to use a higher level of communication, however, when trying to bring agitated inmates into compliance or talk them down from a heightened state of anxiety. Staff are urged not to fall into traps when offenders purposely try to demean, name call, or discredit staff from behind the locked cell door. Given the circumstances, staff may have the option to simply walk away from the situation, unless an obvious threat to security is present, property is being destroyed, or inmates appear to be self-injurious.

Staff actions are being judged by not only the single inmate involved in the confrontation but also by the other offenders living in the housing units, who can see and hear the confrontation. These inmates will be quick to evaluate the staff member's ability to remain professional and to react appropriately without losing composure. Because they are often more familiar with agency and institution policy than many line staff, inmates are aware of the rules. Therefore, inmates eagerly hope to capitalize on an opportunity to recognize staff's failure to follow policy. When this situation occurs, a gargantuan amount of paperwork begins to flow from offenders through the established grievance system and may ultimately result in full-fledged litigation. Staff should be trained to understand that process and be taught strategies for communication and verbal deescalation to prevent these occurrences when possible. Efforts to keep staff in check about retaliating against certain inmates, in passive-aggressive ways, should be reinforced.

In fact, training is key, especially with the support from the facility's leadership. There is nothing that validates the training process more than to see upper management sitting alongside line staff in training rooms. Scenario role plays, where rank is set aside for the moment, will encourage staff and make them feel that upper management really has a sense of what life is like in the trenches.

Conversely, staff should also be trained in understanding the level of approved empowerment and authority they possess over offenders. The level and types of decisions staff can make and impose on inmates should be clearly defined. When supermax inmates are abusive, violent, disruptive, or disobey institutional rules set down in offender behavior codes, staff should feel confident to formally charge inmates with violations. Empty threats, arguments, and shouting matches are never effective. They send a message of inconsistency to the offender population and create tension for other staff. However, when procedures around offender institutional violations are followed appropriately and due process ensues, staff members recognize the effectiveness of the system and their responsibilities to act accordingly.

When all of staff's attempts at gaining inmate compliance have failed, use of force may be the only remaining alternative. Proper training and practice in carrying out the various use-of-force protocols will either resolve the situation safely and quickly or, based on the skill and training of the staff, may:

- further complicate the issue
- lead to staff or inmate injury
- jeopardize the mission
- end in litigation

Current use-of-force lesson plans, taught by highly experienced and credentialed instructors, will help insulate staff from the risks associated with use-of-force incidents that go awry. Training coordinators bear the responsibility to ensure recordkeeping is accurate and up to date and that refresher training is ongoing. When agencies adopt new use-of-force policies, immediate retraining is required. In addition, when planned use-of-force incidents are videotaped and analyzed later, important assessments of staff effectiveness can be made.

Well-defined use-of-force policies are statutorily based. Procedures should be implemented by staff who are trained to react appropriately, using approved, safe, up-to-date equipment. Accurate curricula and well-documented attendance rosters can either support the defense that a staff member was well trained and responded correctly, or they can demonstrate a clear disregard for policy—which means stepping outside boundaries of authority. All training equipment, especially that used in use-of-force incidents, should be inspected frequently and prepared for immediate use. Sound planning should ensure that staff are given hands-on, real-world training in use-of-force techniques.

Monitoring and investigating claims of offender abuse should be swift, and every attempt should be made to authenticate these reports. A zero tolerance policy for violations of staff code of conduct, excessive use of force, or deliberate indifference to managing offenders within guidelines should be the expected response from the top down. Otherwise, offender advocacy groups will encourage class action litigation, or individual inmates will bring suit against anyone remotely related to the incident. Again, proper training will guide staff as they react to various situations requiring some level of force to achieve a safe resolution of the incident.

Even in the best-managed facilities, reports of excessive use of force will surface from time to time. Once investigated, these reports may turn out to be unfounded. However, when investigations reveal that improprieties have occurred, immediate response is required. Historically, correctional agencies have understood that some level of unwritten, silent "code" or allegiance has existed among certain staff. This code may go so far as to take the form of staff protecting, covering up, or lying for one another. Organizational systems that have looked the other way and allowed this code to perpetuate itself unchecked have, during the past few years, been forced to acknowledge its existence and face it head-on. The ability to crack the code in supermax settings is especially necessary. Officers who have been unable to appropriately adjust to the stressors of the job may, when the opportunity presents itself, take illegal liberties with use of force that defies policy.

Subconsciously on the part of the involved staff member, an attempt to angrily impose a personalized form of justice takes over and becomes the driving emotion that influences the behavior. Group dynamics, pressure from peers, lack of checks and balances, or other factors may cause a once, clear-thinking staff member to lose control. In that instance, months or years of frustration, resentment, and a desire to "get even," cause use-of-force tactics to get out of control and result in injuries.

Later, groups of staff may be pressured to "get their stories straight" before writing reports or being interviewed about the incident. When doubt exists about the nature of the truth, formal staff investigations should be opened and additional interviews conducted. Eventually, the facts will be unearthed. This process may take a short or a long period of time. However, the process is never pleasant. Often, a convoluted series of twists and turns resulting in negative staff morale, fear, paranoia, and media involvement rises to the level that interferes with the daily work of the institution. In addition, offenders will exploit those perceived system weaknesses and purposefully pit staff against one another. Accordingly, staff fulfill the prophecy that they are the enemy, are unprofessional, and devalue offenders and their rights.

Supermax administrators who are visible in a facility, model professional behavior, make frequent inmate contact, and visit staff working areas at unannounced times of the day and night send a message that unprofessional behavior will not be tolerated. More to the point, however, prison administrators facing this issue would do well to respond swiftly. They should be open to the investigatory process and use the personnel process to dismiss staff and prosecute them, if necessary. They should perpetuate no secrets and openly provide information to the media and offender advocacy groups.

After an excessive use-of-force incident has been investigated, supermax wardens should establish immediate means to knit a damaged culture back together again. The daily business must be ongoing; therefore, quickly restoring the team and capitalizing on the lessons learned is important. In fact, the warden and his or her management staff will be looked upon to make values-based decisions and create solutions to the problems that are sure to surface during this time. Institutional staff will need reaffirmation about the moral and ethical principles that guide the leadership.

Finally, one of the most important components of any supermax training program is preparing for emergencies. These emergencies may be in any form, from the failure of utility infrastructure, to offender disturbances, taking of hostages, or environmental tragedy. Fire suppression systems should be checked frequently, and staff fire drills should be practiced often. In supermax settings, full offender evacuation is not possible. Therefore, other means of responding to emergencies must be developed and practiced frequently. Issues around staff and offender accountability, operational functions, communications, activation of specialty teams, and so forth should be outlined in formal plans. These plans and related documents, such as mutual aid agreements, should be reviewed at least annually to ensure they are up to date and accurate.

Training-related issues in the supermax setting, as in all correctional environments, are critical. The fundamental principle is simple: the degree of training provided in supermax settings is in direct proportion to the level of safety for staff and inmates—where the goal is a professional, calm environment, and where effective, legally defensible offender management strategies are practiced on a daily basis. Blaming training on each ill-fated event that occurs is common for supermax (as well as other custody levels) administrators. Fiscal and staff support of the training process, quality curricula, and accurate recordkeeping will serve training officers who are challenged to keep everyone happy and out of court.

Balancing Staff Work Ethic with Strategies for Retention

Often, contemporary prison administrators are puzzled about a perceived lack of seriousness that young staff exhibit about the nature of the "work" in correctional settings. Noticeable trends around daily work habits, time and attendance, loyalty to the organization, quality assurance, and so forth seem to be emerging among today's workers. Such behavior appears to be in contrast to the workforce of recent generations. Catchy labels for contemporary workers are surfacing as social changes occur and as new definitions for "jobs" are established. Veteran workers, especially supervisors, are often surprised and irritated at the attitudes younger staff openly convey about the nature of the job, importance placed on leisure time activities, and lack of respect for the chain of command.

Appropriate staff coverage in a supermax setting is critical, and administrators should take care to ensure that the attitudes of the

new work force are successfully integrated with fundamental philosophies of seasoned workers. In the not-so-distant future, experienced prison wardens will retire in large numbers, eventually to be replaced by a new generation of wardens. It will be critical, then, that smooth transitions occur without damaging the facility's mission.

While the dynamics of these generational differences can be observed within correctional agencies, these contrasts should never detract from the organization's goals. In fact, agency strategic plans should map ways to prepare for:

- retaining a suitable workforce whose ideas about prison service are in keeping with the agency's mission
- cultivating a crop of young men and women whose potential leadership skills will be sharpened for future responsibility

This goal may need to be achieved by developing awareness of what makes the new generation of workers tick and moving gradually out of traditional, rigid paradigms.

Flexibility may be common in contemporary, nonprison settings in areas of time spent on task, location of the work, and so forth. For some occupations, this approach to work actually may have extraordinary advantages. The fact remains, however, that structured work shifts, established around offender supervision, have little room for deviation. This idea may be a difficult adjustment for the new generation of workers who otherwise have an abundance of other talents to offer correctional agencies. Attracting and maintaining the kind of workforce needed for supermax supervision in the future may require a thinking-outside-the-box approach. Public safety, however, always will be the number one goal, and the new generation of worker must understand that responsibility.

Staff retention is essential to the facility, as much money, time, and effort have been invested to train and integrate new hires into the culture of the supermax setting. For the new generation of prison worker, incentive programs and awards likely will mean as much as pay and benefits. Agencies may want to consider inducements such as employee wellness, suggestion awards, performance awards, special recognition awards, cash awards, days off, special training opportunities, and so forth. In fact, as the dynamics of various offender types continues to grow more complex, some level of understanding and appreciation for staff stress in the supermax environment is critical. Leadership would do well to create opportunities to measure and address burnout and stress in this special environment.

Traditional referrals to employee assistance resources are a given and should be made as simple as possible. There is no need to add to a staff member's stress by thrusting him or her into a convoluted system where layers of red tape create barriers to acquiring much needed assistance. In addition, therapists, counselors, and other treatment providers should be schooled in the nature of prison work and be familiar with the pressures that are common to such a workplace. Being devalued in the employee assistance process becomes counterproductive and is no help to the employee who wants to do a good job, but who may have experienced a temporary emotional setback. While there may be a variety of reasons influencing this situation, most are likely related to the daily work required in the supermax setting. Staff may not be as engaged mentally and physically in the daily supervision of inmates and operation of all facets of the facility. In this situation, risk increases, errors are common, and inmates quickly capitalize on these vulnerabilities.

Besides traditional referrals for help, correctional administrators may wish to explore other ways to curb or reduce staff stress in the supermax setting. Creative scheduling, post and position rotation, cross training, exercise/workout rooms, or assignments to the supermax prison with specific time–frames may be in order. Some agencies recommend that staff move on to different custody level assignments as a means to keep replacement staff fresh and attitudes unjaded. For agencies having the luxury of geographical flexibility, such a policy may make sense.

Correctional leaders should watch for certain indicators that lead to trends which suggest it is time for staff to rotate out of this environment. Performance reports, use-of-force incidents, inmate grievances, complaints from offender family members, or other visitors, and so forth are all indications that staff are growing restless and losing their professional edge. Is this a poor reflection on the organization or affected staff? No. What it suggests is that the supermax setting is fraught with planned and unplanned events to the extent that the pendulum forever swings from one emotional extreme to the other—often stretching the coping skills for even the most even-tempered and experienced employees. Generally speaking, experienced staff are less likely to openly share with a supervisor that they may be experiencing stress or burnout. The new generation of workers, however, will not only freely share this information but also may willingly leave the organization if the stress becomes too great.

In other words, employee retention and staff wellness go hand in hand toward achieving the goals of the supermax environment. To take care of themselves properly, staff should maintain a balance in their lives by:

- taking care of themselves physically and mentally
- having fun (but fun that does not interfere with work, such as coming in with a hangover)
- eating right
- avoiding smoking
- drinking moderately
- exercising regularly

Staff should attend training courses in wellness to reinforce their efforts to maintain a balance in their lives.

Staff evaluations provide a means for feedback and validate the new generation of worker's contribution to the overall mission.

These evaluations should be used more often than just the once or twice a year requirement. In fact, staff evaluations can be used as tools for mentoring, coaching, nurturing desired work habits, and monitoring improvements—all useful for those supervising the new generation of worker.

In addition to a system that rewards employees, reminders about the professional obligations inherent to all law enforcement personnel should be reinforced. When staff are known to take liberties with, or violate standards of conduct because they feel immune to their rule, swift correction is required, tailored to the nature of the offense. When correctional administrators lead by example, they are respected for their ability to balance an environment where rewards for outstanding behavior are obvious and discipline for inappropriate actions is properly invoked. Then, and only then, will workers demonstrate respect for positions of authority and value the fundamental principles that are the organization's framework.

Conclusion

Correctional administrators have long believed that staff are an organization's greatest asset. Accomplishing strategic goals and objectives to maintain the integrity of the mission is only possible through the efforts of the men and women who, each day, knowingly place themselves in harm's way to preserve the safety of the public. Supermax prison staff face unique daily challenges due to the management strategies required for the offenders housed there. The propensity for violence on the part of these offenders requires the staff who supervise them to be the "best of the best" to manage the "worst of the worst." Being prepared to deflect offender manipulation, being skilled as a master oral communicator, cultivating mutual support and teamwork, as well as using decision-making power and authority appropriately— these are just a few of the skills needed to function effectively in the supermax setting.

Recruiting and hiring such workers takes planning and aggressive tactics. Correctional workers must be willing to understand that traditional prison operations do not fit within either the realm of the physical plant, or program design of the supermax prison. In fact, staff hired for this environment must be willing and able to take new and different approaches to offender management. Something as simple as library book distribution to inmates becomes labor intensive and requires a number of security safeguards to be integrated into the process.

Staff who are observant during welfare rounds, appear and act professional, follow the rules, and are fair, firm, and consistent will gain the respect of the supermax offenders. These staff generally will have an easier time adjusting to the rigid, stress-filled atmosphere. Coworker relationships become strong, and inmates are less inclined to resort to violent behavior when staff stay on a path that is principle-centered and defensible.

The supermax prison environment offers agencies a safe and modern option for managing its most violent offenders. However, the critical link to the program's success is staffing thoughtfully, ensuring that training and professionalism are constantly reinforced, maintaining zero tolerance for incompetent employee performance, and providing consequences to bad behavior. Finally, supermax staff should be openly valued and recognized for the dangerous work they perform to maintain the mission of public protection.

Chapter 5: Technology and the Supermax Prison

Donice Neal
Warden
Arrowhead Correctional Facility
Canon City, Colorado

Introduction

Inmates are masters at finding ways of defeating security systems. Interestingly, the inmate's goal of defeating the system is a major inducement for causing improvements in the security system. From one standpoint, inmates are our best advocates for improving our systems and processes. With their infinite ingenuity and considerable time, they are the motivators for prison administrators and staff to find new and better ways of conducting business. Inmates cause us to be more aware of our surroundings and environment, to look for problems before they happen, and to tighten our security to protect the community, staff, and other inmates. They remind us that we must constantly find new and improved methods to protect security systems from breaking. Nowhere is this practice more important than in a supermax facility, where staff are in daily contact with violent predatory inmates. These inmates are not only violent and predatory but also intensely dedicated to "breaking" the system.

From another standpoint, inmates in a supermax setting offer us the greatest potential to fail in our most important goal of protecting the community and staff. If proper security systems are not in place or if they fail, a dangerous and often violent situation can occur quickly. Anyone who has been involved in a violent prison incident is aware of the importance of good security. Inmates test security, and staff must be ready to pass the exam. In sum, the population of violence-prone inmates offers a great challenge for correctional staff to constantly look for and resolve potential security problems.

Current technological advances have an enormous effect on prisons. Technology can create a safer environment, enhance security operations, frequently save operating costs, and improve staff morale. However, technology is more than machines, correctional toys, or bells and whistles. Any discussion of security technology must include the staff who use and maintain it. To be effective, technology must be properly tested and well maintained. Staff must be trained on its use, operation, advantages, and limitations. Maintaining and reinforcing good security practices must be an ongoing goal. Only when staff realize their importance and their impact on safety can technology be used appropriately. People are ultimately responsible for making technology succeed or fail.

Technological System

Technology is not just a single piece of equipment used to prevent a security breach.

To be effective, technology must use a system of interconnected and integrated strategies. Redundancies and overlap should be built into the strategy, so that when one system fails, another automatically takes its place to protect the breach. For example, a "man down" alarm cannot replace the control officer who has a direct line of sight. Interlocking gates with control panels in separate secured control centers provide security back up to protect the facility when one control center is entered by hostile inmates. In this instance, the inmates can go no further than the immediate unit. Security systems should operate in layers at least two and sometimes three deep. All critical areas must be protected in depth. One system can be defeated; however, redundant systems provide insurance that back up will be available when and where it is needed.

Broadly speaking, security technology systems can be divided into these categories:

- perimeter security systems
- internal detection
- locks and locking systems
- communication
- monitoring and surveillance
- biometrics
- fire/life safety
- nonlethal weapons

When agencies select security technology systems, facility mission, cost, effectiveness, failure rate, false-alarm rate, maintenance, demands on staff time, ease of use, site location, policy, and facility design all must be considered for the program to be effective.

Perimeter Security Systems

Perimeter systems are basic to prisons. The public rightly imagines fences and towers when it thinks of prisons. Fences are typically the first level of security in a prison and range from rock walls to lethal electric fences. However, a fence is not just a fence. Numerous types of fences, alarm systems, and detection devices must be combined to provide efficiency for the site and design of the facility. In designing a secure, integrated perimeter security system, these issues must

be considered:

- type of fence(s), lethal verses nonlethal
- razor wire
- detention systems/alarms
- lighting
- clear zones (areas with no visual barriers or physical access)
- rat barrier (concrete barrier beneath perimeter to secure the fence to prevent inmates from digging underneath it)
- anticlimb material (wire mesh/cloth attached to the fence to prevent inmates from getting hand-holds to climb fence)
- perimeter patrols
- gates
- towers
- tower officer and weapons
- communication systems

Each aspect must be carefully evaluated as to its advantages, disadvantages, and capability to integrate systems to provide a unified, effective perimeter operation. To maintain an adequate level of security, fences around supermax facilities should use at least one alarm system, rat barrier, anticlimb cloth, razor wire, and clear visual sight lines.

Numerous types of technology will enhance the security of a perimeter fence. Perimeter detectors consist of switches strategically located around a perimeter. The most used switch is a microwave technology one that has a microwave transmitter which emits high frequency radio waves. The radio waves form an electrical field. Anyone entering the field disturbs the radio waves and triggers an alarm. Other types of perimeter alarms are electric field sensors, seismic in-ground sensors, video motion detectors, infrared sensors, and so forth.

All perimeter detection systems have false alarms that vary depending on the terrain and location of the facility. Animals entering the electrical field, objects blown into the protected field by wind and weather conditions can cause nuisance alarms. All alarms must be checked by security staff. Checking alarms can be irritating, especially when there is reason to believe the alarm is false. Therefore, perimeter detection systems should be evaluated prior to selection to ensure that the system selected is the best system for the site. A careful assessment of the advantages and disadvantages for the location and specific terrain should aid the agency in selecting the system that will produce the fewest false reports.

Developing a security technology committee also would aid the agency in selection and assessment of equipment, site needs, and facility needs. The security technology committee—consisting of corrections staff who perform research, testing, and specification requirements—ensures the most efficient use of available resources. Standardization of technology allows economy of mass purchasing and superiority of performance as all equipment is evaluated and tested prior to purchase. This method prevents costly "mistakes" of obtaining products that may not perform at the level reported, may not fit the intended need, or may require excessively high maintenance. Additional efficiencies are obtained through shared knowledge and training in the use and repair of available technological resources. A consultant may be useful in helping a facility evaluate its needs and aid in the selection of the best product based on the budget.

Recently, several states have elected to install a "lethal fence" around high-security perimeters. The lethal fence is an electric fence that carries up to 10,000 volts of electricity. The fence is positioned between the perimeter fences to form a physical and psychological barrier around the facility that is formidable both to unauthorized persons attempting to enter the facility or inmates attempting to escape. The lethal fence has a record of high reliability and can defeat resistance. Some of these fences can be programmed so that they normally operate in a nonlethal mode. In this mode, the fence shocks the intruder with a time delay that switches to a lethal mode. This delay feature protects birds and small animals that have accidentally entered the fence area from being electrocuted. While installation of the lethal fence is costly, it replaces some of the need for towers and staff for the towers, thereby paying for itself very quickly.

For example, the lethal fence constructed at the Sterling Correctional Facility in Colorado cost $1.7 million to build. The fence replaced the need for five towers, saving Colorado $1.2 million in construction costs. Therefore, the money saved from not building the towers paid 70 percent of the cost of the fence. The real savings, however, is the estimated $750,000 per year in reduced staffing costs. In one year of operation, the fence paid for itself.

In addition to electronic technological systems, human resources must be considered. Maximum-security and supermax facilities should establish posts in which staff can observe and/or quickly respond to an alarm. The towers are elevated posts usually located on a perimeter and typically staffed by an armed officer. Towers are positioned to give a clear view of the perimeter, so that staff can clearly observe activity in the area. In addition to tower posts, perimeter patrols should be established.

Perimeter patrols consist of an armed officer who drives while continuously observing the perimeter of the facility. Potentially, perimeter patrols may be more important than tower posts because patrols have the capability to respond to a problem area outside the fence. The ability to move provides more flexibility to a system than the tower post and aids the correctional officer assigned to the post in maintaining a state of alertness. Communication capability among the perimeter patrol, control center, and towers is essential. Communication will heighten alertness and keep all staff assigned to the safety and security of the perimeter properly informed of any issues or situations.

Internal Detection

While a perimeter fence is very observable, imposing, and often creates a psychological and a physical barrier to the facility, internal detection cannot and typically should not be seen. Internal detection systems protect seldom-used spaces in a facility, such as mechanical rooms, and protect exterior and interior doors, ventilation openings, windows, ceiling crawl spaces, and so forth. Therefore, internal detection systems report an intruder entering a secure location. Internal detection systems also should be used in high-security areas such as the armory and locksmith shop.

The basic principle of intrusion-system operation is that when a person enters a protected area, the intrusion is detected, and an alarm is sounded. Systems include alarms that break an electrical circuit or a light beam, or detect sound, vibration, motion, or change in a capacitance or electrostatic field. These systems should alarm in several fashions and locations but always alarm in the control center.

The advantages and disadvantages to each system require careful evaluation to determine the technology most suitable to the facility. Designs are numerous with advantages and disadvantages for each situation. This is another area where a security consultant or a security technology committee would be a valuable resource. A few common types of alarm systems include the following:

- electrical circuit system
- light beam intrusion system
- sound detection system
- motion sensors, ultrasonic or microwave sensors

The electrical circuit system typically provides trouble-free service with few nuisance alarms and is usually adequate in low-risk situations. This system can be costly to install when there are numerous entry points to the protected area. Light beam intrusion systems use a light sensitive cell and a projected light source. When the light beam is interrupted, an alarm sounds. This type of detection is useful in portals or driveways and if it is used properly, affords an effective, reliable notice of intrusion. Sound detection systems can be used effectively to safeguard an enclosed area, such as a vault or warehouse. Sound detection systems use supersensitive microphone speaker sensors and are installed on walls, ceilings, and floors of protected areas. Any sound caused by attempted entry is detected by a sensor. This type of system can be easily and economically installed, but it cannot be used in areas where high noise levels are encountered or outdoors. Motion sensors use ultrasonic or microwave sensors in an interior area and detect a Doppler shift in transmitted and received frequencies when motion occurs within the protected area. Motion sensors provide effective security against intruders concealed within the premises.

All intrusion systems should alarm to a control center that is staffed twenty-four hours a day. Because they are less susceptible to animals and the environment, interior intrusion alarms have far fewer false or nuisance alarms than perimeter alarms. Even though internal alarms are less vulnerable, they must be physically checked and tested with checks and tests logged on a regular basis.

The introduction of contraband is related to intrusion systems and the desire to prevent access to restricted areas. Both focus on the prevention of unauthorized introduction of products, weapons, or persons into the facility. Most people are familiar with metal detectors in all airports and many courthouses. With the occurrence of terrorist attacks, metal detectors can be expected to become an even more familiar sight. Metal detectors are also common sights at facility entrances and other strategic points. Walk-through detectors are electronically equipped archways that sound an alarm when a person walking through is carrying more than a designated amount of metal. Handheld metal detectors are battery-operated, portable devices that detect the presence of metal. Handheld detectors are effective in pinpointing the location of the metal triggering the alarm. With integrated and consistent use, these devices are effective in preventing the entry of traditional metal weapons. Again, however, the most important link to maintaining good security is the correctional officer.

X-ray machines or fluoroscopes are absolutely essential in preventing contraband from entering a facility. These machines detect not only metal but also currency and drugs inside packages or products received. To be effective, these machines must be used at one centralized location to examine every item entering a prison including food, office supplies, linens, inmate property, and inmate mail. Fluoroscopes are also beneficial for performing cell searches. Inmate property, mattresses and pillows, and anything movable can be loaded into laundry carts and taken to be examined in the fluoroscope. This process provides a more thorough search and saves staff time. An added feature that is invaluable is the capability of programming images of objects into containers for training purposes or for assessing staff awareness of what they are seeing. The machines show certain objects in containers at certain times. If staff do not perceive the object or report the object's presence, they are not as observant as the post requires. The machines also compile data of various examples of contraband, again for training purposes. The effectiveness of this technology depends on the diligence of the staff who operate the equipment. Therefore, staff must be attentive and aware of the importance of their position in preventing contraband introduction. They should view their efforts as a challenge to keep their prison free of contraband.

Locks and Locking Systems

The key is the single symbol that characterizes the prison setting. Plaques are made for retirees using the key to symbolize their career in corrections, and nicknames are given to correctional officers based on key operations. The key is the ultimate symbol of the control that staff exercise over inmates. The importance of the key is clearly evident in prison operations. When agencies develop a locking system, they must consider the following:

- key control systems
- required redundancies
- integration of various aspects of the system and other security systems
- location and use of sallyports
- electrical versus manual key control or both
- type of door or gate operation
- maintenance requirements
- key exchange process and accountability
- food ports
- door position indicators
- inventory/accountability process

Locking systems can be manual, mechanical, or electrical-mechanical. Each category of locking system is efficient and serves its purpose well. Manual locking systems use people to physically pull a lever or turn a wheel to lock a door. Manual locks require someone to manipulate the lock each time the door is opened. Mechanical locking systems are similar to manual locking systems except one lever or wheel may operate a series of doors from a remote location. Electrical-mechanical systems perform the same function as mechanical systems, but the door operation is activated by an electrical device. Door operation also can use compressed air or pneumatic power for movement.

When electronic door operating systems are used, they must be designed to fail (secured doors and locking devices automatically lock when electrical or computer systems fail) in case of malfunction. Doors may either swing or slide. Sliding doors offer the most security and allow time for staff to react to and to correct errors. Swinging doors require less space and time to operate. They may be opened from a remote location, but cannot be closed remotely. If a swinging door is accidentally unlocked, staff have no time to correct the error. The door is open, and the inmate may exit through the open door before staff can physically respond to shut the door. Because the door may be closed, but not locked, an electric indicator panel with colored light indicators showing locked or unlocked door positions is necessary.

The most important factor with locks and locking systems is to practice good key control. Keys should be inventoried and accounted for at all times. When taking custody of keys, staff should accept responsibility for the keys by exchanging an identification tag or chit for the keys issued. In addition, staff should verify the number of keys assigned to the key ring, and check the condition of the keys. When keys are turned in at the end of the day, the same process should occur with the officer accepting the returned keys. Keys should be maintained in the facility with an emergency back-up set at another location. The officer issuing the keys should inventory keys at the beginning and at the end of each shift.

In addition to maintaining a first-rate control and inventory of keys, the facility must develop an inspection and maintenance system to ensure that keys and locking systems are in good working order. The schedule should require the locks to be tested at least weekly if not more often. This inspection should include all perimeter gates and internal door locks. Door and door operations also must be tested. System problems should be immediately reported to the locksmith for repair. All broken, damaged, or unusable keys should be destroyed by the locksmith, and remnants should be taken off site of the facility for disposal. Adequate inspections require communication with the locksmith who is responsible for maintaining the inventory of keys and key blanks, and keeping all the keys and locks in good working order. In addition to the scheduled inspections of keys and locks, the locksmith should visually inspect and inventory key rings at least quarterly.

Communications

During any training seminar or management meeting, the one area always listed as the single most important issue for the agency is communications. There cannot be too much communication or too many ways of communicating in a maximum-security or supermax prison. Communication must extend in all directions. There must be written and nonwritten communication between staff and inmates, security staff and programs staff, security staff and administration, support services and medical staff, visitors and staff, and all combinations. Communication must be timely. In a high-security operation, staff need to have information immediately to respond appropriately. Communication includes information gathering and sharing that information with all staff who may be affected.

Information can be exchanged through numerous technologies. Many of the technologies are standard to prisons but no less effective because of their wide use. One of the most common technologies in information sharing is the FM radio. Radios may be handheld or installed in a vehicle. Handheld radios are two-way radios that enable staff to talk with each other or with a control center while moving through the facility. These radios can be preprogrammed to communicate with various groups and are most effective when the facility has the capability of communicating with other local law enforcement. The radios also may have emergency alarms.

Vehicle radios are similar to handheld radios but typically are installed in security vehicles and perimeter vehicles.

Telephones, cellular phones, and intercom systems allow communication between specified locations. Electronic technology has improved these systems. Telephones can be programmed to perform group calling and automatic call-back for emergency situations. In these situations, the telephones are programmed with staff home phone numbers. Staff on emergency teams are all automatically called by engaging the system. The phone will recall those individuals who were not reached during the first try. This feature enables staff to be notified of emergencies and to respond more quickly with fewer staff needed to make the notifications.

Phones also may be programmed to perform as duress alarms. There are two basic methods of programming the phone for a duress alarm. The phones may be programmed to provide an off-hook alarm.

Simply put, an employee can remove the receiver from the phone cradle and after a specified number of seconds, the location will be alarmed in the control center. The second method is a "crash line." One specified number dialed will notify the control center of a problem and the location of the problem.

Personal duress alarms allow staff to send signals to the control center when an officer is down or when an emergency arises. When users perceive a threat, they press a transmitter button or it may be automatically triggered when the device is tilted beyond a specific angle. Once activated, the system relays critical information about who is in danger and where. Typically, these alarms about the size of a pager are worn by staff. When staff are assigned to work in isolated areas, a panic button system can be installed. When these wall-mounted buttons are pressed, they send an alarm to the control center identifying the location of the problem. Combined with video monitors, duress alarms provide a quick assessment of and fast response to staff who are in trouble. To ensure that alarms are functioning as designed, the personal duress alarm system should be tested at least quarterly. In addition, the personal alarms should be tested in various areas to ensure that the system is accurately reporting the location of the alarm.

Technology is also useful in monitoring inmate communication. Inmate phone systems should have monitoring and recording capability. This system is essential to intelligence gathering. Despite notification that calls are being monitored, inmates regularly tell friends or family about assaults or other events, plans to introduce contraband, or escape plans. Modern inmate phone systems can even allow staff to hone in on key words and phrases, and defeat third-party calls. By monitoring these conversations, staff learn the who, what, and where necessary to maintain control or prevent a crisis.

Intercom systems are useful for monitoring conversations between inmates in the housing units. In addition to monitoring inmate conversation, intercoms aid in communication between staff and inmates. Inmates can express their needs to unit control staff who can respond to questions or needs. Finally, a closed-circuit television system is an excellent method of delivering information to inmates about programs, policies, and changes occurring in their environment. Innovative program staff also can safely provide a host of programs to educate and keep inmates productively engaged during their confinement. Some systems are experimenting with allowing inmates to have keyboards that enable them to communicate with selected staff and complete assigned lessons.

With today's perimeters being almost impenetrable, most correctional staff will agree that inmate escapes or hostage situations are likely to occur during a transport. During this time, little technology or support is available for backup in case of an emergency. The public is most vulnerable to incidents involving an inmate during this time. Video conferencing is a viable alternative that allows necessary inmate court appearances, parole board or immigration hearings, or medical evaluations to occur without the risk of the inmate leaving the secure environment. With this technology, video images are digitally transmitted over phone lines to a remote location. The technology allows the inmate to interact with the judge, the physician, the parole board chair, or other service providers without risk to the community. It may be used to reduce the number of inmate transports, reinforce security objectives, and reduce the presence of inmates in the general civilian population. Therefore, it produces cost savings through reduced transportation, vehicle use, fuel, and staff overtime and through reduced administrative and logistical efforts to schedule and move inmates.

Managing information is important for the efficient operation of a prison. In our technological society, an increasing amount of data is being compiled that must be managed. Systems must be developed for offender classification and tracking, resource management, and maintenance of equipment. Easily retrievable information gives a clearer picture of individual inmates, inmate groups or gangs, medical problems, and program needs. Staff can rapidly retrieve inmate information and intelligence to determine the risk of incidents in specific scenarios and, thus, make better decisions. With enhanced and increased information, staff can better manage the inmate population without incident.

Again, alert, conscientious staff are the single most important element to a secure and safe prison operation. Possibly the most important aspect of preventing problems and creating a safe environment is good staff/inmate communication. A first-rate officer will take the time to explain the reasons for requests or rules, ask how inmates are doing, and be aware of when the inmates are experiencing personal problems. Inmates who believe these officers are fair and concerned are more likely to inform the officers of violence or escape plans. This type of communication may save the lives of both officers and inmates. Through communication rather than through brute strength the officer interacting with inmates gains true power and control. Therefore, it behooves all correctional staff, especially staff in a maximum-security or supermax prison, to use their communication skills as effectively as possible.

Monitoring and Surveillance

Considerable overlap exists among communication systems, locks and locking systems, internal detection, and monitoring systems. Some of the same technologies overlap to provide benefits to other areas of security. For example, motion detectors, especially those with video monitoring capability, are used not only to prevent intrusion into a secure area but also to visualize events occurring in a remote location. This overlap meets the need for redundant systems and should be carefully considered in establishing a security program.

Closed-circuit televisions may be used to monitor living unit day halls, living unit access, sallyports, pedestrian circulation corridors, elevators, and other key points within a facility. Closed-circuit televisions consist of television cameras placed in potentially vulnerable and/or strategic areas that are monitored on a television screen usually by staff in a control center. Depending on the location, covering the camera with a smoke-colored plastic dome may be necessary to prevent visitors, inmates, or intruders from knowing where the camera is focusing. Additionally, administrators should take care to prevent a correctional staffer from observing an excessive number of monitors. Too many monitors cannot be adequately watched and can cause mediocre security practices. Then, the position and location of the monitors in front of the officer is important. Monitors must be placed so that they are neither too high nor too low. They must be positioned so that the officer may easily and clearly see them without glare from the windows or lighting. Audio monitors provide a function similar to the closed-circuit television, but rather than transmitting a visual image, they transmit audio sounds to locations where correctional staff are. Existing public address systems may be modified to perform this function.

Audio-video cameras are simple, inexpensive technology that is invaluable in maximum-security and supermax settings. Video cameras provide a record of activities, such as use-of-force incidents and emergencies, as well as continuous monitoring of inmate areas. All planned uses of force, such as cell extractions, must be videotaped. This practice provides clear documentation that protects staff against claims of abuse. Knowing that the incident is being videotaped may also provide a psychological deterrent and prevent an employee from overreacting with more-than-necessary force. Supermax facilities maintain a high level of public and media interest. A range of special interest groups: inmates, advocates, lawyers and others frequently challenge their policies and file lawsuits. This one piece of technology along with clearly thought out policies that are practiced and enforced can do more to safeguard the facility than any other.

Additionally, a video camera system that is constantly monitoring and recording inmate activities provides a deterrent to negative or criminal inmate behaviors. Such a system has been proven to reduce these behaviors in controlled housing units. While supermax facilities are sometimes described as the end of the line for inmates, most inmates do not want to be on video recordings involved in activities that will result in additional prison sentences. Therefore, a video recording system assists in making the environment safer and more secure.

Access control systems allow designated persons to enter secured areas while preventing entry of unauthorized persons. These systems may consist of a pushbutton type of locking device where only those authorized entry have the combination. Card readers or "Smart Cards" also can be used for the same purpose. These systems not only limit entry into designated areas but also establish a record of entry. The record created enables staff to determine who entered the restricted area at critical times. Because they can easily be reprogrammed if lost or damaged, the systems have an additional advantage over the more traditional key locks.

Biometric Technology

Biometric technology is an automated method of measuring a living object quantitatively. The technology is based on the fact that every person has physically or behaviorally measurable characteristics unique to each individual that can be exactly measured, numbered, counted, or otherwise quantified. While once thought of as science fiction, biometric technology is becoming a common element of everyday life. Biometric technology is being used to add a level of security to identify and authenticate users in many trades and endeavors. Biometrics is commonly used in the banking and travel industries, for computer security, to gain entrance into housing and apartment complexes, and by the military for multiple functions. In corrections, where a primary portion of the job is identifying and tracking inmates, biometric technology should have an increasingly significant impact. It is not unheard of for inmates to switch identity with another individual and walk out of a prison. Biometric technology can ensure identification is accurate and monitor all individuals entering and leaving facilities.

Biometrics has two basic functions. The first function is identification and answers question, "Who is this person?" The second function is verification and answers the question, "Is this person who he or she claims to be?" Identification and verification have distinct functions. Identification is when a subject's identity is determined by comparing a measured biometric against a database of stored records. It is a one-to-multitudinous comparison. Because the database for comparison is much larger, it is a more time-consuming process than verification. Verification authenticates the user's identification. This usually requires an individual to make a claim of identification by presenting a code such as a PIN number. With verification, biometrics makes a one-to-one comparison between a measured characteristic and one known to come from a particular person.

Biometric systems are numerous and measure such characteristics as fingerprints, facial features, iris, retina, hand geometry, palm, voice, signature, wrist subcutaneous vein patterns, keystroke dynamics, body salinity (salt content), body odor, thermal facial images, acoustic head resonance, and ear formation. Such measurements as body odor recognition, thermal facial images, and acoustic head resonance are uncommon in use due to the expense, impracticality, or lack of effectiveness. However, other systems are very reliable, cost effective, and practical. In general, the less intrusive the measures are perceived to be, the more they are accepted by users.

Most biometric systems have three components including the following:

- a mechanism to scan and capture an image of the person's unique measured characteristic

- a system to compress, process, and compare the unique characteristic to the stored characteristic
- a method of interfacing with an application system

For example, if a palm reader is used to identify and/or verify individuals, the system would need a mechanism to scan, store, and compare the stored data.

The most practical and successfully implemented biometric technologies are those using optical measurements of the iris and retina, hand geometry, and fingerprints. Iris and retinal biometric systems are more accurate than hand and fingerprint measurement systems. Optical systems have more characteristics to measure and identify than other technologies. However, the technology tends to be more expensive to install, tends to be more cumbersome to use, and is viewed as more cumbersome and intrusive by those using it. Additionally, optical scanners have more difficulty reading biometrics of people who are blind or have cataracts.

Fingerprints have been used in criminal justice for many years. Measurement of fingerprint characteristics are viewed as the least intrusive while still remaining reliable. Consequently, fingerprint identification systems are probably the most popular and widely used form of biometric technology. Hand geometry biometrics involve scanning the shape, size, and other characteristics of some or all of the hand. Hand geometry or palm print scanners nearly match fingerprint scanners in terms of reliability, but the units tend to be much larger in size and cost than fingerprint scanners.

Whatever the technology selected, all persons entering the security perimeter of a supermax facility should be scanned into the system and then identified each time they enter or leave the facility. This includes inmates, visitors, and correctional employees. Additionally, level of reliability should be considered and an acceptable level determined. Most biometric systems have a variable threshold or sensitivity setting to enable

the user to determine the level of reliability accepted. There are two types of errors in biometric systems. The false rejection rate (FRR) is experienced when a user's biometric data is rejected by the system. The system falsely determines the user is not who he or she claims to be. The effect of a too high FRR is an inconvenience to the user and a tendency to ignore the rejection. If security is set too low, the user experiences a false acceptance rate (FAR). This is potentially more dangerous, because it allows the wrong individual to clear the system. FRR and FAR are inversely related. As FRR goes up, FAR goes down. As FAR goes up, FRR goes down. To use the system most effectively, FRR and FAR must be balanced in terms of sensitivity.

Life Safety

Fire can be devastating in a prison system. Nowhere is this situation truer than in a maximum-security or supermax setting that is designed to be difficult to exit and houses predatory inmates over whom staff have a responsibility for safekeeping. There are two basic types of fire systems. Alarm systems are activated when they detect fire or smoke. With this system, staff may be required to extinguish the fire. Suppression systems mechanically control the spread of fire. Both systems are necessary for the safety of inmates and staff.

The simplest alarm device is the manual pull station, a common device in public places. Anyone observing a fire or smoke pulls the lever to notify fire authorities of the problem. The alarm warns of the fire, closes fire doors to prevent the spread of fire, heat, and smoke, controls ventilation and air handling systems, and releases extinguishing agents. Heat detectors react to a rapid change in temperature. Smoke detectors react to invisible particles caused by combustion.

Fire suppression systems may be manual extinguishers, fire hoses, or sprinklers. Extinguishers form the first line of defense because they are portable and easy to operate. Extinguishers are automatic systems that apply water to the fire. No system is adequate unless staff are carefully trained to respond. Staff must have training on using fire extinguishers, including when and on what type of fire they can be effectively used. Six types of fire extinguishers should be available:

Water—Water is the most common fire extinguisher and can be used when the material on fire is wood, paper, cloth, or fiber.

Dry Chemical or Carbon Dioxide—These extinguishers work well against flammable liquids such as paint, paint thinner, gasoline, oil, tar, solvents, fats, grease, and electrical components.

Halon—Halon extinguishers are appropriate for use against fires involving ordinary combustibles, flammable liquids, and electrical equipment.

ABC Combination—The ABC Combination fire extinguisher can be used against class A, B, or C fires. These are fires fed by ordinary combustibles, flammable liquids, or electrical equipment. Ratings are based on the size and type of fire to be extinguished.

Dry Powder—Dry powder is used to blanket combustible metals such as magnesium, titanium, or sodium potassium alloys.

Foam—Foam may be used to extinguish fires involving ordinary combustibles and electrical equipment.

Staff must be trained and drilled on the use of safety gear that provides protection if they are required to enter smoke-filled areas. Self-contained breathing apparatus must be readily available to staff and in sufficient quantities to assist in the event of a fire.

Additionally, staff must be trained on and regularly practice evacuation processes, including route, and locations. In a maximum-security or supermax setting, areas should be predetermined to enable partial evacuations. One area should be designated, along with several as back-up areas. Administrators

must regularly schedule drills so that each employee immediately knows how to respond to a fire alarm.

To further enhance the safety of staff and inmates, administrators must take care to determine allowable inmate property. Property should be limited in amount and type. Excessive amounts of property increase the fire load of the facility, providing extra fuel to burn. Furnishings must be nonflammable to the extent possible.

One issue that should be evaluated is whether to authorize smoking in the facility. Many prisons have become nonsmoking facilities, and we strongly encourage this practice. Prohibiting smoking not only creates a healthier environment but also eliminates many fire hazards. While smokers will protest, in the long run, staff and inmates both will be safer.

Nonlethal Weapons

While every effort must be made to prevent unnecessary force, situations arise where nonlethal force may be the safest manner of resolution. Officers often may find themselves in a position where they cannot protect themselves, other staff, or inmates from injury without the use of a nonlethal weapon to help control the situation. In some situations, staff must quickly assess the situation and determine the safest method of resolving an incident—verbal exchange, commands, or force. In other situations, staff action is prescribed by regulation. In all these situations, staff must be concerned about the safety of those around them and resolve the incidents with the least disruption to the facility. Nonlethal weapons commonly used include chemicals, electronic devices, and batons. They are not recommended for everyday use or as standard equipment for the officers.

Law enforcement personnel have used batons since the nineteenth century. No picture of the English bobby is complete without a billy club. Batons or truncheons are versatile tools used for several purposes including as impact weapons, for disarming or immobilizing violent individuals, self-defense, leverage and pain compliance, or riot control. Batons typically are about three inches in diameter and of different lengths. They may be made of wood, polycarbonates, plastic, or metal. Styles vary based on preference, training, and intended use. They may be rigid, have a side handle or be expandable. The type of baton used should be standardized, and staff must be trained and/or certified on the specific piece of equipment.

Chemicals are a more recent form of nonlethal technology designed to enhance the safety of operations. Historically, chemicals have evolved through CN (chloroacetaphenone), commonly known as tear gas. CN is used to gain control through a burning sensation in the eyes that causes tearing and burning in the throat and nose. CS (ortho/chlorobenzal-malononitrile) is considered more potent than CN; it causes pain in the throat and chest, and nausea and vomiting. CN and CS have largely been replaced by OC (oleoresin capsicum). OC, a derivative of cayenne pepper, is commonly known as pepper spray. OC is an inflammatory agent that causes the eyes to tear and involuntarily shut. After being subjected to OC, an individual's airways swell, and he or she may experience coughing, gagging, gasping for breath, and a burning sensation on the skin. A major advantage of OC over CN and CS is the ease of decontamination through breathing fresh air and washing the subject with cool water. Its effects last approximately twenty to forty minutes, giving staff ample time to gain control of violent, unruly inmates. Although the effects are similar on most people, occasionally a person will be resistant. In such cases, another type of nonlethal force may be required.

Electronic devices are lightweight weapons or shields that carry an electrical current when they are activated. When the probes make contact with the skin, an electrical circuit is formed, and the person loses neuromuscular control. Electronic devices are often effective on persons who do not respond to chemical agents or who are using drugs.

Staff must receive extensive training before using any nonlethal weapons. They must be trained to use the proper weapon for the particular circumstance, and be able to assess when and how to effectively use each tool. Specific regulations and procedures must be developed to provide clear directions, prevent abuse, and protect the employee in case of lawsuits. These tools for controlling a violent or potentially violent situation are best used by highly trained teams who work together as a unit in practiced drills.

The Human Element

This chapter has emphasized the importance of staff to security. The best way to improve security is to have well-trained, security-minded staff. Technology systems may indicate the presence of a problem, but in the end, the personnel intercept and resolve the problem. The question then becomes what can be done to help improve the response of personnel, increase the safety of staff and inmates, and reduce the threat to the community? The answer is to ensure that staff have the tools to help them do their jobs effectively. This goal can be achieved to a certain point through the use of the various technologies reviewed. The best way to improve safety in the facility is through security tests, searches, audits, training, proper maintenance of equipment, and regular inspections.

When working the same job day after day, staff easily can become oblivious to security issues or problem indicators. They see the same door daily and grow to expect it to be in a certain position. They grow so used to seeing that door that they do not see when it is off center. They also check to see that the door is secured time and time again. It then becomes easy to assume that the door is secure because it always has been secure. In other words, it is easy to get careless. Inmates in a supermax facility watch for that laxness and are quick to take advantage. Therefore, having the security practices and physical plant audited by someone outside the facility is important. Fresh eyes often see things missed by persons working within the environment.

Ideally, two audits should be conducted each year. An internal audit should be conducted by security-minded staff to identify areas where security can be improved. The second audit should be conducted by persons who do not work at the facility. The audit should be thorough and include information on what needs to improve or change, and provide suggestions on how to improve each deficit in security. Following the audit, a plan of action should be developed and efforts made to improve each deficit found.

Training and education is extremely important for staff to function at peak ability. The operations in a supermax facility differ from other facilities. The needs and expectations of staff differ. Use of force takes on greater dimensions than in lower-custody facilities. And most important is the great need for ethics and integrity in an environment that is often tense and abusive for correctional officers. In this environment, it is not unusual for the line officers to be called foul or obscene names, to be spit on, or to have urine, other body fluids, or other foul substances thrown on them. These individuals must be trained to respond in a professional manner to these types of situations. Staff should have input into their training needs. Training plans should be developed in conjunction with training personnel to ensure staff needs are met. Efforts should be made to give staff pride in their performance as professionals. Training in communication skills is essential for career development, to provide alternatives to physical force or to calm a situation, and to enhance the safety of the officers. Knowing how to communicate effectively is frequently the best method of preventing a major incident.

In addition to training in professionalism and communication skills, staff must receive training to enhance their safety in a poten-tially dangerous situation. At a minimum, staff require training in first aid, operation of self-contained breathing apparatus, self-defense, forced cell entry, legal issues, use of force, and essential security procedures. Training must be ongoing so that it is ingrained and staff react without thought or hesitation. Finally, the training program must be evaluated and modified every year to ensure that staff are receiving the most accurate, up-to-date information.

To ensure that staff are able to respond quickly in an emergency, practice drills must be conducted. Drills can range from accounting for all staff or inmates present to detailed exercises specific to a particular emergency situation. Drills should be conducted on all shifts and include exercises for as many types of emergency situations as can be developed. Types of emergency situations should include the following:

- hostages
- hazardous material spills
- utility failure
- employee strikes
- natural disasters
- escapes
- riots
- fire
- threats of hostile takeover

During each exercise, staff auditors should be assigned to note responses both positive and negative. Involved staff should be debriefed to provide further information for improved future performance. Staff should be made aware that the exercises are not pass/fail situations but learning situations to improve their skills as correctional personnel.

Security tests occur on a much smaller scale. These exercises involve specific tests on security systems and note the alertness, observation, and quick response of the tested employees. For example, an item of clothing may be placed on a perimeter fence to test how quickly perimeter patrol personnel notice it. Contraband can be programmed to show in a container as it passes through the fluoroscope to test staff's alertness to the items examined. A tool can be removed from the tool room to test inventory processes. Such tests should be simple and be treated as a learning device rather than a pass/fail situation. Staff should be recognized for their accomplishment when tests are successful. Although staff may at first believe that the administration is trying to "catch" them or make them fail, they typically develop a sense of pride as they learn that they can "pass" tests. They also will quickly become more aware of what is taking place around them. Their alertness and skill at performing their job becomes another source of pride and builds morale.

Technology is not useful if it is not in good repair or does not work. A preventative and predictive maintenance schedule should be developed to prevent breakdowns and extend the life of the equipment. Life safety and emergency equipment should be tested at least quarterly to ensure proper functioning. Equipment failing preventative maintenance tests should be included in plans of action to correct or replace the failed item with well-functioning systems.

Finally, the physical plant should be inspected regularly. Inspection schedules should be developed and followed. For example, perimeter gates, locking mechanisms, mechanical devices, restraints, and control devices should be checked for breakage, malfunction, and ease of operation at least weekly. Predesigned checklists are a good method of accomplishing this task. Doors, windows, bars, grillwork, fences, grates, and hardware should be checked daily. Checks should be logged and verified. To be effective, useful, and used, equipment must work consistently on demand, and staff should have a sense of security that when necessary, they can depend on functional devices.

Summary

The statement "good security is not convenient" is most true in a maximum-security or supermax setting. Staff must follow security practices to achieve a safe operation. Technology is a critical issue in corrections. Correctional personnel need to evaluate, select, and use technology as a valuable tool to enhance the safety and security of the facility. Technology is typically expensive. To make the best use of limited budgets, agencies should carefully evaluate purchases to ensure that the equipment best meets the needs of the agency and specific facility. Despite the benefit to operations through the use of technology, never forget that staff are the key to effective and efficient operations. The ultimate concern of correctional employees is public safety. Staff should take pride in this and their actions should be guided by this mission. Therefore, we must provide personnel with the tools required to reach a constant state of preparedness to succeed in their mission. We must constantly assess our procedures, be open to change, be prepared to react to any situation presented, and always remember that technology is an aid, not an answer.

Chapter 6:
Use of Force in Supermax Prisons: Setting the Example

Eugene E. Atherton
Assistant Director of Prisons, Western Region
Colorado Department of Corrections
Canon City, Colorado

Introduction

Supermax prisons serve jurisdictions by managing a large percentage of the dangerous and disruptive inmates. Normally, more than 50 percent[1] of the supermax population has committed assaultive acts or threats to commit assaults against staff or other inmates. Many have significant, long-term histories of assaultive behavior. Not surprisingly, despite staff efforts to peacefully resolve issues, a higher frequency of uses of force occur in supermax prisons than in any other correctional setting. Correctional officers find it is not only their responsibility to deescalate volatile issues with inmates but also necessary to use physical force with confidence when other means of control are not appropriate.

This last characteristic, the need to use force, in the supermax environment attracts the attention of the media, courts of law, and adversarial citizen groups. Specific supermax programs are criticized by those who highlight serious problems in the use of force in managing inmates. Their concerns are outlined in legal decisions or in negotiated agreements as a result of out-of-court settlements.

Use of force is one of the most important acts of the correctional profession, performed under the most difficult and demanding conditions. Therefore, the remainder of the correctional community often looks toward supermax employees' performance as a model for the profession. Whether it goes well or results in failure, it sends an influential and unmistakable message to the inmates, to other correctional professionals, and to the public.

Legal Issues

The major legal issues related to use of force in supermax prisons are similar to those in other areas of the law related to corrections. Sometimes within the framework of a legal decision the judge makes comments that are not a conclusion of law or finding of fact but a pronouncement of principles that are important to the case. Those principles are, at times, as important as findings of fact and conclusions of law, and agencies should take them seriously when operating or planning for the operation of prisons. The following three sets of principles are essential when agencies consider use-of-force programs in the supermax environment:

- In *Madrid v. Gomez*[2], and within legislation in state systems, correctional staff are clearly empowered with a duty to use force. In *Madrid v. Gomez*, the court said that there is no question that this demanding and often thankless undertaking (managing high-security inmates) will require staff to use force against inmates. Indeed, the responsible deployment of force is not only justifiable on many occasions but also absolutely necessary to the security of the institution.

- In *Madrid v. Gomez*,[3] the Federal District Court referred to high-security, supermax-type environments when it said: "The prison setting offers a tremendous potential for abuse. Custody personnel are in constant contact, day after day, with a difficult, frustrating, and sometimes openly and actively hostile inmate population. They also have powerful weapons and enormous manpower at their disposal, and exercise nearly total control over the inmates under their supervision. Adding to this volatile mix is the fact that the prison setting and particularly the SHU [Security Housing Unit] is far removed from the usual sights and sounds of everyday life. From the outside, the SHU resembles a massive concrete bunker. . . . The physical environment thus reinforces a sense of isolation and detachment from the outside world, and helps create a palpable distance from ordinary compunctions, inhibitions and community norms. If, in addition to all of the above, prison administrators fail to adequately supervise and monitor the use of force, the potential that force will be misused increases significantly."

This author's experience and those of others who have worked in the supermax envi-

ronment fully agree with this concept. It is clear that courts of law expect oversight and supervision to be sufficient for these conditions.

- In *Bell v. Wolfish*,[4] U.S. Supreme Court Justice Thurgood Marshall said that "the greater the imposition on detainees, the heavier the burden of justification on the government." The foundation of the law on Fourteenth Amendment due process protections related to corrections is primarily one of concern with physical restrictions. Due to the highly restrictive level of confinement, correctional staff in a supermax setting have a higher degree of responsibility to ensure the safety of inmates than in other correctional environments, and to justify and support with documentation acts related to placing, managing, and retaining inmates in supermax confinement.

The messages contained in those statements are very clear. We have a duty to use force in a manner where professional conduct is ensured through careful management of the process. Another way of looking at it is that we, as correctional practitioners, must be the best under the most demanding circumstances.

In *Madrid v. Gomez*,[5] the court provided additional messages and helpful suggestions concerning the essential elements of a use-of-force program. A system that adequately monitors and regulates the use of force consists of five components:

1. written policies that clearly identify for line staff when and how much force is appropriate under different circumstances
2. training of correctional officers about the proper use of force
3. supervision of the use of force to ensure that it is consonant with departmental and institutional policies and procedures
4. investigation of possible misuses of force
5. officer discipline for the misuse of force

Finally, the courts have been helpful in providing guidelines to assist in evaluating uses of force for the possibilities of abuse. In *Hudson v. McMillian*,[6] the court offered five criteria for determining whether the use of force was appropriate or inappropriate— "whether force was applied in a good faith effort to maintain or restore discipline, or maliciously and sadistically to cause harm." The five factors to be considered include the following:

- the extent of the injury suffered
- the need for the application of force
- the relationship between the need and the amount of force used
- the threat reasonably perceived by the responsible officials
- any efforts made to temper the severity of the forceful response

The guidelines, directions, and conclusions of courts of law with respect to supermax-type confinement apply as the rules that must be followed to receive favorable outcomes upon review and to get closer to doing the right thing in the eyes of the world. Attorneys have described use-of-force issues entertained by the courts as the most popular issues today attracting legal attention. If we do not demonstrate efforts and successes at compliance, we will certainly lose control of the substance of our programs to the successful arguments of the plaintiffs and the courts.

Use-of-force Philosophy

Most uses of force in supermax environments go well and are done professionally. But expectations that staff performance will support and reflect the direction of the agency mission and policy are sometimes unfulfilled by disappointing staff performance. Serious cases have caused major challenges for correctional systems across the nation. Often, the content of the philosophy and how it is communicated at all levels of the organization (through policy or organiza-

tional culture) leads to the disparity between mission and performance being increased or minimized. Nowhere in corrections is philosophy more important than as it relates to uses of physical force in gaining compliance from resistive inmates. Where failures occur, organizations are normally found in violation of the boundaries of their mission, and they often face unkind judicial and media scrutiny. The incidents related to use-of-force experience in jails and prisons are well known across the country. They are normally catastrophic in terms of impact on the organization and are, at times, a reflection of the culture and fabric of the organization during the time of the incidents.

Generally, philosophy may be defined as a theory or fundamental beliefs related to or forming a basis for an activity. Some commonly used terms and phrases described in policy and curriculum related to use-of-force philosophy include the following:

- Be professional, present an appropriate behavior model to inmates/detainees, staff, and the public. Ensuring that staff recognize the direct relationship between mission accomplishment, staff professionalism, and staff performance in interactions with inmates is critical.
- Use only the amount of force necessary to gain compliance. Any greater amount, when accompanied by other supporting information, may be judged as malicious rather than a simple error in enthusiasm.
- Minimize injury. Staff need to remember that all force applications should be designed and operated to minimize injury.
- Do not personalize conflict with inmates. Once staff allow an inmate to influence their personal feelings in the form of insults or reference to families, the inmate receives a clear advantage in the relationship.
- Avoid playing into the games inmates or detainees are trying to play. We know many of the inmates in the supermax environment suffer from personality

disorders that are characterized by depending on power relationships during interactions with others. When officers join in the "I win, you lose" game, uses of force begin to take on very negative connotations.

- Deescalate conflict whenever possible. The higher a conflict escalates, the more likely force will become necessary, and the more likely injury will occur.

- Assume a nonegocentric attitude that focuses attention away from staff and onto the inmates' conduct and the need to appropriately resolve problems. The author's personal experience and the experiences of others is that this approach makes sense and is most often effective.

- Employ the use of time whenever available. Whenever a hostile experience takes more and more time to resolve, the chances for a safe and effective resolution increase.

- Do not punish but effectively manage. When staff direct derisive or unnecessarily personalized comments to inmates during use of force, the ability to successfully manage over the long term is significantly decreased.

These elements indicate that the skill of applying physical force does not stand alone among the skills correctional staff are expected to use in meeting the challenges of managing inmates. After training, staff often come away feeling confused by all the messages. However, the ideal world expects correctional staff simultaneously to be prepared to achieve a cooperative, voluntary compliance from inmates/detainees and use physical force at any time it appears reasonable based on the circumstances of the moment. It is undeniable that the two are strongly related and not separate and independent approaches in managing inmates/detainees.

The officer who initiates physical contact in a use-of-force incident is very often the one who will serve food trays or hand out mail to the same inmate on another shift. Poor use-of-force decision or technique can have a long-lasting negative affect in relations with inmates. In the worst case, it can get people seriously hurt. At times, correctional staff feel the unfortunate inflexibility to favor one approach over the other in their relations with inmates.

Some take pride in their expertise in using methods of physical force and feel great value in being available when it appears that there is a need to use those skills. In a correctional setting, these persons are highly valued for their courage and skills. In some jurisdictions, the leadership may submit to temptation to strongly reward those staff without ensuring that the individuals are accountable for their performance. Unfortunately, some in that class place less importance on being good at gaining voluntary, positive cooperation from inmates during routine duties prior to resorting to physical force. At the other end of the spectrum are those who feel their expertise is using a variety of skills to deescalate conflict and solve problems without relying on physical force, or threats of physical force, to achieve a positive outcome. Some perceive these individuals as violating professional boundaries in relationships with inmates (getting too close) and think that they may not be depended on to perform well when the circumstances require the use of physical force.

In this author's opinion, the ideal correctional officer is capable of using the skills all along the spectrum extremely well. He or she comprehends the circumstance of the moment and makes sound, mature decisions concerning managing relations with inmates. However, when all appears equal, the officer should err on the side of safety and control of the moment. Requiring staff to take unreasonable risks to avoid using physical force is unthinkable. Professional presence is usually well respected by inmates and is normally very effective in achieving voluntary cooperation.

The officer with professional presence feels balanced and comfortable in using all the skills on the spectrum and moves comfortably from one response to the other. This type of officer usually manages job-related stress very well. Under emergency conditions, the officer is comfortable in assuming a leadership position to make good decisions and take decisive action. People can learn to perform in this way. Correctional agencies must pass such a level of quality on through training and role modeling to others. Correctional agencies must train and develop staff to perform with confidence and clarity of direction at all locations on the spectrum.

Force Options Used in Supermax Prisons

The following discussion will provide examples of the force options typically available for use in supermax prisons. These options are reasonable choices depending on the type and extent of resistance presented by the inmate, the overall factors of the confrontation, and the staff members' perception of the incident.

Officer Presence

This force option is used to gain voluntary inmate compliance through the presence of officers among the inmate population. The continuous appearance of properly uniformed, competent, professional-appearing staff are always an influence on an inmate's decision to resist direction or act inappropriately. The presence of staff, and the issue of specific numbers of staff, have been the basis of many debates concerning appropriate staffing levels in jails and prisons. In addition to having enough staff to accomplish the major work tasks in an area, the need for staff to establish a presence to provide attention directly to inmate conduct on an ongoing basis too often is ignored. The causes of many correctional disasters have included the absence of officers in inmate work, living, and program areas. Some of the more publicized correctional emergencies in the form of inmate assaults or riots have occurred in high-security or supermax settings. The after-action analyses point directly to the failure of

systems and the unfortunate consequences of cutting corners on resources and job performance.

Experience has demonstrated that wherever you leave inmates unsupervised, dangerous contraband appears. Inmates then begin to compete for informal leadership, and the area becomes a location for inmates to conduct illegal activities, including assault. The inmates' perception of the officers' authority and power can be enough to change offender behavior. For example, consider a supermax environment where officer presence is limited due to staffing shortages or attention to matters other than those that encourage inmate contact. Control over inmates and the systems that ensure safety begins to deteriorate immediately. Under those circumstances, staff are encouraged to take shortcuts on basic security and safety techniques.

Verbal Direction

This force option is the verbal direction by an officer that achieves compliance from an inmate. Many difficult situations may be resolved by good communication skills, problem-solving strategies, verbal direction properly delivered, methods of approaching hostile inmates, deescalation techniques, and acute sensitivity to early warning signs of problems among inmates.

Much of the success of this method lies in the officer being able to provide communication without further escalating an already tense condition. Often, this type of officer is experienced, well respected by the inmates, and they do not personalize their communication to any specific person or group. In the supermax environment where the inmate is likely to be restrained or in a confined space, the additional aspect of time works in favor of the officer achieving compliance from the inmate. Both officer presence and verbal direction appear to be appropriate where inmates are offering various types of verbal and psychological resistance.

Physical Force

There are many force options in this category. There are empty-handed control options, such as pain compliance, joint locks, and leverage locks. These choices are appropriate for low-level physical resistance. When encountering highly threatening resistance, officers should consider using more aggressive options, such as neck restraints, strikes, OC gas, electronic control, and impact weapons. These techniques and devices are neither designed to, nor do they typically cause serious bodily injury or death. This category represents the vast majority of the force options typically used in supermax prisons.

Lethal Force

Lethal force is expected to typically cause serious bodily injury or death. It is normally authorized for use when all other force options are ineffective, and to protect a person from serious bodily injury or death, or to prevent an escape of a convicted felon. It is commonly used in supermax prisons where escape attempts are discovered or where there is a serious and imminent threat of serious injury or loss of life. Those conditions normally occur during inmate assaults involving weapons. Given the large array of force options and techniques for solving problems and gaining voluntary compliance, this author believes that lethal force should be rarely used in supermax prisons.

Typically, supermax prisons provide an exceptional amount of structure and systems for every task completed in daily operations. When those systems are ignored and abbreviated, inmates see an opportunity to behave in an aggressive, violent manner. Under those circumstances, often in instantaneous segments of time, staff must make reasonable decisions in the selection of force options—based on the factors of the confrontation and their perception of the incident.

Extended Use of Restraints

In the face of extremely threatening or dangerous conduct by inmates, where appropriate policy and practices exist, managing inmates in restraints for prolonged periods of time is sometimes reasonable. Under no circumstances should inmates be subject to extended periods of restraint using security-type restraint equipment (handcuffs, belly chains, leg irons, and so forth). Only clinical restraints (canvas, rubber, leather strapping related to four-point beds, and similar devices) should be used for those purposes. Under no circumstances should inmates be subject to restraints as punishment. Without the proper checks and balances in policy, punishment too often may be disguised as a need for control.

The frequency of resorting to this type of force varies depending on the type of inmate population at each correctional facility. However, supermax prisons tend to experience a large number of inmates in this category of behavior. Most commonly, restraints are used to manage self-destructive behavior. Commonly, enraged inmates who are confined to their cells may try anything to be self-destructive, including behavior such as head banging, eye gouging, hanging, or cutting themselves with any object they can find. Makeshift approaches such as taping their hands (they often injure themselves with metallic restraints), or trying to persuade them to wear a protective helmet are seldom successful. Under those circumstances, the use of specially designed restraining equipment is a welcome relief to everyone and major assistance in ensuring the safety of the inmates. Because this measure to control inmate behavior is highly aggressive, it normally is accompanied by strict procedure, very specific documentation, and frequent supervisory reviews at multiple levels of authority. Although the measure usually involves all inmate management staff, depending on the preference of the jurisdiction, the process may be directed by either security personnel or clinical services staff. During extended periods of restraint, the inmate's well-being should be frequently monitored by medical staff. Frequency of monitoring should be determined based on the inmate's medical history, mental health, and extent of restraint.

Policy covering the prolonged use of restraints must include the type of restraint to be used. Soft restraints in plastic or leather must be the choice where more long-term, aggressive behavior is anticipated. The restraints can be attached to a bed specifically designed for that purpose or the inmate can be left in a cell where the restraints are not attached to a stationary fixture.

All the specifics with respect to placing inmates in restraint for prolonged periods must be expressed in policy. The following are some important elements recommended for inclusion in the policy. The inmate's critical functions such as breathing, blood circulation, and other medical concerns must be fully and continuously addressed. Both medical and security staff must provide and document frequent reviews and evaluations of the inmate's condition. Mental health personnel should provide direction or consulting advice on the decision to remove restraints. The initial decision to restrain and subsequent decisions to restrain for prolonged periods of time must be authorized by the shift commander or a higher level of authority. Extended periods of restraint (four to eight hours) must be approved by departmental executive staff. As with all applications of all types of force, correctional staff involved in the use of restraints for a prolonged period of time must be fully trained in the procedure.

Specialized Teams

Correctional staff must be prepared to make reasonable selections of force options based on the factors of the confrontation and their perception of the circumstances of each event. Some duty posts are assigned a lethal weapon in the control room, towers, and in transportation vehicles. Under other conditions, staff must be prepared to use lesser force options at any time during the operation of a correctional facility. Many jurisdictions have specialized teams of staff who

exercise the uses of force under specific, non-routine conditions. There are a variety of configurations throughout the profession. Too often, new construction and prison architecture of supermax prisons cause staff to become complacent in thinking that the physical plant will provide all the security needed. The history of disturbances in high-security settings proves these teams to be as important today as any other time in the past. The following sections describe examples of these teams.

Forced Cell Entry Teams

The forced cell entry team has not always been a common practice in corrections. Years ago, staff were not trained. There was little or no protective equipment. Staff improvised cell entries, with a resulting high incidence of staff and inmate injury. Current practice in supermax prisons is much more safe and effective. Forced cell entries are typically more common in facilities that manage high-risk, aggressive offenders or in those facilities that are not being effective in using other, nonphysical means for solving problems with offenders. Reasons for forced cell entry include the following:

- Ensuring safety. For example, an inmate covers the window to his cell and cannot be observed. Officers enter the cell to ensure that he is safe and not harming himself.
- Transporting an inmate to the shower, court, and so forth.
- Removing an extremely disruptive inmate to "time out" outside the cellblock to minimize disruption to other inmates.

More recently, agencies have resorted to using Oleoresin Capsicum (OC) after all verbal attempts to resolve problems have failed and prior to the order for the forced cell entry team to enter the cell. Sometimes, the team is held in reserve, out of sight of the inmate, while the OC is being administered. OC is a highly pressured gas that is directed into the inmate's cell. Inhalation of OC causes irritation to the eyes and lungs, causing the inmate to become physically compliant. For inmates who are causing the scenario for their own entertainment or to boost their prestige among other inmates, the drama of forced cell entry is lost with the use of OC. It is no longer seen as activity for the inmate's amusement. For those reasons, the use of OC can reduce the frequency of forced cell entries by as much as 50 percent.[7] Particularly with the advent of the transmittal of disease through body fluids, reducing the chances of violent staff/inmate contact, where possible, is an important policy matter.

A forced cell entry team is a group (four to six officers) that has been specially trained in providing a preplanned, organized process for gaining cell entry for retrieving a disruptive or noncompliant inmate or moving an inmate through the use of force. The team should be equipped with protective equipment for all members. The team should be qualified and prepared to use the type of nonlethal force option that is reasonable given the factors of the confrontation. Once the team is presented to the inmate, he or she may become cooperative in response to the presence of the team. Otherwise, the inmate normally is restrained through empty-handed control or strength techniques as the team members enter the cell. Most teams will use a reverse curve, Plexiglas shield, or stun shield held by the point person as the team enters the cell. The strategy is to pin the resistive inmate against the cell wall as the remaining team members gain control of the inmate's arms and legs, with each team member responsible for a specific limb.

Typically, forced cell entry is used to prevent an inmate from being self-destructive; to prevent the destruction of property; to move inmates according to administrative or court order; to vacate a cell for operational purposes (sanitation, searches, emergency evacuation, and so forth); and to attend to an ill or unresponsive high-risk inmate. Normally, most forced cell entry experiences occur in high-security environments.

Except in emergencies, this process should not take place without the following:

- training for team members beforehand that includes specific roles and certified training for each weapon used
- extensive efforts to persuade the inmate to comply
- videotaping for the record
- permission from a higher authority to proceed
- thorough documentation from all present
- consultation by medical staff

Forced cell entry may be complicated. There should be specific plans for overcoming wet or soapy floors, inmate attempts at jamming doors, various barricades, possible weapons held by the inmate, and methods of ensuring successful insertion of OC into the cell prior to entry.

Emergency Response Teams

An emergency response team (ERT) is a designated, specially selected and trained team at a correctional facility or complex that is used to contain and control an emergency (riot, fire, natural disaster, and so forth). Normally, participants are volunteers and are not provided additional compensation for their efforts and commitment. Teams typically are organized according to the level of force they are trained to use. Emergency response teams often are designated as lethal force/weapons teams, riot control teams, and cuffing/retention teams. Typical emergency response mission requirements are to do things such as:

- disperse groups of rioting inmates
- apply all levels of force
- conduct searches
- provide escorts for staff, inmates, and mutual aid agencies
- administer first aid or CPR
- perform staff welfare checks
- supervise inmate holding and triage areas
- establish/supervise perimeters

Specialized Tactical Teams

A specialized tactical team is a designated, specially selected, and trained team (such as SORT, Special Operations Response Team, and SWAT, Special Weapons and Tactics) that usually services an entire system to contain and control special types of emergencies. Normally, participants are volunteers from facilities across the jurisdiction. The team is highly trained in specialized applications of force. Other specialized teams such as fugitive search, hostage negotiation, and post-trauma treatment may exist in some systems. Members must be trained and experienced in performing their roles within the context of the emergency management program. All of these teams play a significant role in managing emergencies in a supermax environment.

Planned Use of Force

Staff must be expected to apply force immediately at any time while performing their work in the supermax environment. Sometimes, they must act suddenly. Some examples include breaking up fights; encountering an inmate who becomes angry, aggressive, and unwilling to comply with direction; or moving or transporting inmates under restraint. Other times, the inmate is isolated and the immediate area is secure, allowing the passage of time to support further attempts at resolution or to plan and coordinate the use of force.

Planned uses of force help ensure a greater degree of success and safety throughout the incident. All planned uses of force should be coordinated with a higher authority, be videotaped for the clearest possible record of the event, and accompanied by extensive nonphysical efforts to resolve the issue. Medical staff should be in attendance throughout the process. Finally, after the event, the administration should conduct a review of the entire incident.

Force Deployment

Generally, any force deployment in supermax systems should be a practiced procedure that each agency operates—based on a balance between the perception of risk presented by inmates and the need to secure force-related equipment properly. The majority of agencies keep storage of weapons, munitions, and emergency response team equipment in a secure space outside the facility perimeters. Storage spaces and systems should be arranged to achieve maximum efficiency in quickly deploying equipment to authorized staff.

Agencies employ a variety of approaches. Many facilities operate satellite storage spaces within the facility for faster deployment of equipment. Some operate posts with lethal weapons capability on perimeters, in interior yard spaces, and even in housing unit control rooms. Some agencies allow officers to carry intermediate control devices (J-sticks, OC canisters, electronic devices, and so forth) inside the facility on a routine basis. Others require that the equipment be drawn from a protected storage space, when necessary. For example, in one major urban jail system, emergency response team equipment is stored on a cart kept in a secure location. Under emergency conditions, it is wheeled to the general area before staff draw their equipment and begin to engage the emergency. All systems should include accountability steps through matching inventories for checking out and then for returning weapons to storage spaces.

An inmate can inflict mortal wounds with a homemade knife or a blunt object in a matter of seconds. Those sorts of assaults are not uncommon in a supermax environment and lives can be saved by quick, professional deployment of force. However, others may argue that too much dependence on uses of force causes the focus to shift away from critical inmate management activities, such as communication, dialog, or face-to-face problem solving. Each side of the discussion should realize that both approaches are compatible and should coexist as effective approaches to managing inmate populations depending on specific circumstances.

Implications of the Excessive Use of Force

Most experienced professionals and legal scholars believe that due to the adversarial nature of the supermax environment, unregulated, unsupervised uses of force by staff ultimately will rise to some measure of abuse. Therefore, being aware of the implications of excessive use of force is important. Some of those implications for a correctional organization are the following:

1. Staff involved in an excessive use of force may be required to respond to criminal and civil allegations and are likely to be subject to severe disciplinary action by their agency.
2. Excessive use of force models behavior to other staff. This means that some may view violations of and inconsistencies in following laws and rules acceptable within the organization. Such a condition promotes an unsafe and unpredictable atmosphere for everyone.
3. Excessive use of force models behavior to inmates that communicates a message of acceptance of unlawful force as a primary method of solving problems among humans. This message is directly contrary to the mission expressed by most correctional jurisdictions.
4. Excessive use of force may be viewed by staff as an acceptable substitute for the array of interpersonal skills that are critical to effective inmate management.
5. If excessive use of force is used to manage inmate behavior, it is likely to affect staff/inmate dialog in an extremely negative fashion. This condition can distort communication and raise fears and feelings of unpredictability among inmates.
6. Excessive use of force may informally place a perception of power in the hands of participating staff. That power is likely to be inconsistent with intentions of the formal organization. This condition can create divisive and unhealthy relationships among staff in the form of staff taking sides of those who participate and those who do not. Staff who choose not to participate may appear withdrawn and uncommunicative, and they may resign or apply for transfer.
7. Excessive use of force easily can combine with other facility problems (ineffective communication, insufficient programs, and poor staff morale) to ignite an inmate disturbance.
8. When inmates witness staff using excessive force or corporal punishment, they may decide that their environment is no longer safe and they may be encouraged to take measures to protect themselves.
9. Public knowledge of excessive force incidents is extremely damaging to the image of corrections professionals and to the careers of those involved. It can create long-term regulatory entanglements through courts of law and by human interest groups.

Key Indicators of Excessive Use of Force

The national survey in *Use of Force: Current Policy and Practice*[8] clearly indicates that in all uses of force reported there were very few reports of instances when the force used was excessive. In addition, very few disciplinary actions were taken against correctional officers for excessive use of force. This finding is consistent with research concerning uses of force by law enforcement agencies. Thus, correctional staff overall are doing an excellent job.

However, it does not mean that excessive force and corporal punishment is not occurring. The policy, procedures, training, and practice of using force in a supermax prison environment must be a process that is constantly monitored. Correctional leaders must remain diligent and proactive in their sensitivity to each use of force within their organization. Without that effort, a failure occurring in the system may be only a matter of months, weeks, or days. Part of that process must involve being aware of some of the early warning signs that excessive use of force may be happening in the organization.

Nowhere in corrections does the saying, "where there is smoke, there is fire" apply more than in the review of information on use of force. The following are some indicators that excessive use of force may be occurring. Should any number of these indicators exist, leaders (superintendents or wardens) should expend greater effort to examine related incidents at their facility. The indicators include the following:

1. Staff and/or inmate rumors, incident reports, and inmate grievances may be important indicators. This situation does not suggest that leadership should react to every individual piece of information. However, when patterns evolve from numerous sources, the possibilities cannot be ignored. The administrator should look for a pattern that he or she feels is substantial enough to prompt a formal investigation.

2. When unexplained injuries occur during the course of a use of force, they merit careful attention. These injuries must not be related to preexisting medical conditions and must not fit the factors of the confrontation. For example, a forced cell entry is conducted, and it goes well with moderate resistance on the part of the inmate. However, serious injuries occur that seem excessive under the circumstances. As a result, further examination may be needed.

Some examples of those kinds of injuries are deep and extensive lacerations; breaks in large bones (such as the leg or arm); or bruising from hard, intermediate weapons that appear to be excessive for the circumstances or in locations which suggest that the inmate

may have been fully restrained at the time the blows or strikes were delivered. Where these instances occur in a pattern, serious and immediate examination of the events is important. A pattern could be more than two consecutive events in a relatively short period of time. A single occurrence would warrant examination should the circumstances include severe injury and absence of significant justification. In the event death occurs in association with any use of force, an official investigation will occur. All aspects of officer performance and decision making will be carefully examined by the department and most likely a court of law.

3. When an increase in the frequency in the overall uses of force occurs without a reasonable explanation, management should remain concerned until an explanation is given. The increase could be overall or more focused on one shift rather than others.

4. Management should be aware that a higher potential exists for excessive use of force where there is a history of burnout and no rotation of staff in facilities—such as supermax prisons that contain high-risk, disruptive inmates, and a higher potential for failure in relationships with inmates.

5. Management should be sensitive to the idea that excessive force possibly is being used when: staff fail to provide sufficient information, are clearly mimicking one another on incident reports, or are reluctant to discuss conditions surrounding a use of force.

6. Likewise, staff should be sensitive to significant and extreme changes in inmate behavior. An example would be when inmate behavior is uncharacteristic, such as: inmates no longer participate in normal communication; larger numbers of inmates show up for sick call; inmates group themselves by race or gang affiliation; there is a significant increase in requests for transfer in jobs or to other facilities. Uncharacteristic behavior also

may include usually calm, relaxed inmates becoming very verbal and aggressive, or usually communicative inmates becoming suddenly withdrawn. Under these circumstances, staff must trust their hunches and make a special effort to communicate with inmates and other staff.

The negative effects on individuals and organizations of a pattern of use of force as corporal punishment can be very difficult to undo. At times, the challenge can assume the dimensions of an attitude change throughout the entire organization. In the most extreme cases, the challenge can be attempting to change a culture of terror—where genuine concern over the welfare of inmates has been replaced by hatred, contempt, and indifference to that of a new way of doing business.

Element of a Successful Use-of-Force Program

The key components of a successful use of force program for corrections include, at a minimum, administrative oversight, training, policy, and documentation.

Administrative Oversight/Full Disclosure

All security, emergency, and staff performance systems in corrections must be monitored and supervised continually. Uses of force may be reduced significantly by staff who invest time and energy in analyzing inmate populations to predict where problems may occur and suggest improvements specific to those areas. Without constant attention, these systems can deteriorate and produce major problems within days or weeks of a change in focus. Administrative oversight must lead to a clear understanding among staff that the leadership of the organization is supportive and confident in their use of force as a part of their job performance. Staff must know that reasonable use of force is their duty and the right thing to do. At the same time, administrators should encourage staff to accept accountability for job performance. This accountability needs to include tangible support for excellent work, constructive criticism toward improving future performance, and assurances that staff will be treated fairly. The results of a system of this nature will produce many official pronouncements of praise as well as descriptions of where performance should be improved. The process must be perceived as a partnership in the operation of the use-of-force program. Staff fears are usually not fully satisfied except through the personal experience of working in a system that achieves the objectives described in this paragraph.

The advantages of an effective administrative oversight system include the following:

- It delivers a critical message to the entire facility or department and the public indicating that each use-of-force incident is an extremely important event which is taken seriously. The related oversight is an expression of that importance.
- It provides a written history of force incidents, which serves as educational information, a security-performance measurement or indicator, and protection from legal and administrative actions.
- It provides an opportunity for management to express support and confidence in staff performance when they use force.

The essential elements of administrative oversight include:

- The administrative review is openly complimentary towards excellent staff performance in the use of force and provides constructive direction for improvement, where appropriate.
- All staff and witnesses to uses of force must produce a written description of their observations, and the staff involved must be interviewed as part of an administrative review. An additional, standardized use-of-force report should be completed to accompany the staff statements. The national survey in *Use of Force: Current Policy and Practice*[9] indi-

cates that only 59 percent of the corrections/detention departments require a formal, written statement, and only 53 percent require an interview with the officers involved. Without the full participation of officers in the use-of-force review, the importance of the process is seriously diminished.

- It involves a review at multiple points within the agency. At a minimum, it should include the shift commander; an administrative officer; the administrative head of the facility (such as a warden or superintendent), and at least one executive level person from the central agency administration (for example, an inspector general, a deputy director of prisons, the county sheriff, or a chief of security operations). One level should include a formal review with formal taped interviews with involved staff, examinations of all documents, videotapes, and related information. This review should conclude with a formal written report and findings to the administrative head of the facility. All information should be shared and discussed with the staff involved in the interest of improvement and professional development. The administrative head of the facility should review the information and formally declare, in writing, that the amount and type of force used was appropriate for the circumstances. If it was not appropriate, the follow-up corrective measures should be a part of the documentation. The remainder of the reviews should be informal with questions and requests for clarification addressed to the administrative head of the facility.

- The information reported on the use-of-force information report should be standardized and support a larger system of data gathering. Types of information included might be frequency of force incidents by facility, department, shift, and so forth. That information must be used by correctional management to track critical trends or characteristics on use of force. The results should guide the design of future training, applications of resources, and strategic plans for future objectives.

- Decisions must reflect on the unique factors of each incident. However, administrative review should provide aggressive approaches and outcomes for excessive uses of force in terms of disciplinary and corrective actions. These decisions must follow when staff clearly use force in a malicious manner, solely intended to harm without mitigating, legitimate concerns related to maintaining security and preserving order. Accountability cannot exist without clear, predictable consequences for wrongful actions. These decisions are always difficult and must be made in light of all the circumstances. However, the outcome must provide a clear message to all that such abusive acts will not be tolerated under any circumstances. Without that message, the integrity of the use-of-force program will be at risk. Without that message, some staff will see the condition as a green light to formulate their own style of implementing uses of force separate from and independent of the department.

- The administrative oversight must have integrity in that each incident is viewed with the same level of seriousness and attention to detail. The process must never be viewed as a rubberstamp exercise.

- The administrative oversight process must be clearly expressed in policy.

Training

Use of force programs in supermax prisons cannot operate successfully without sufficient staff training. A few years ago in a midwestern state, inmates in a close-custody portion of a prison created a disturbance. During the process of bringing the incident under control, several staff were injured. Afterwards, one of the uninjured staff was interviewed by the media and asked what contributed most to his remaining injury free.

He immediately responded by saying that his safety was a result of instinct strongly shaped by training which guided his actions during the disturbance. It seemed to him as though his actions were automatic.

As the national survey indicates in *Use of Force: Current Policy and Practice*,[10] most agencies train staff in use-of-force policy, equipment, and techniques. Use-of-force training must achieve several outcomes. First, and most important, training must guide staff performance towards compliance with policy, procedure, and departmental standards. Appropriate staff performance should be second nature, and staff should feel a high level of confidence in their ability to perform under a variety of circumstances.

Second, use-of-force policy should shape staff thinking. Attitude is everything, and there is no place where that idea is more important than in use of force in corrections. The training forum is the most effective tool for setting the tone for the professional use of force. That process must require students to have an understanding of the philosophy and principles underlying the use of force. It must require students to have an understanding of the relationship between the mission of the department and the concept of professionalism in the use of force. Students also must have an understanding of the direct connection of both to staff performance in their relationship to inmates. Finally, this process must address the code of silence in terms of outlining the legal liability of staff for not reporting acts of excessive uses of force. Additionally, the negative effects on the organization should be reviewed.

Third, training must help staff achieve confidence in applying force and help them feel comfortable in going directly to the best force option. Each use-of-force option is shown on the use of force wheel on page 81.

The force wheel places the officer in the middle facing a variety of types of resistance that could be presented by inmates. The outside rim details the force options available, depending on the nature and extent of the resistance. Contrary to the use-of-force con-

tinuum, the force wheel emphasizes that the officer must make instantaneous decisions based on the circumstances of the moment. The officer is not able to follow a neatly ordered progression of decision-making along a continuum.

Other important issues related to use of force training include the following:

- Training in use of force needs to provide explanations of important definitions such as physical force, control, resistance, and corporal punishment. Departments should include their definitions of these terms in their use-of-force policies. Correctional officers need to have the same understanding and use the same terminology when referring to force issues.

- The training needs to include a method of relating force options to the types of resistance and risk presented by an inmate in a supermax setting. The force continuum is a graphics tool to demonstrate how force options change with the rising or lowering of risk and resistance presented by the inmate. The misconception created by such devices occurs because the continuum is presented as a sliding scale. Some corrections staff feel encouraged to attempt to perform or extensively consider all lower levels-of-force options prior to applying the appropriate level of force. Many corrections professionals claim that this method, compounded by a vivid emphasis on legal liability, may cause officers to be more resistant rather than decisive in proceeding to the correct force decision. Training must help staff achieve confidence in applying force and feel comfortable in going directly to the best force option considering the factors of the confrontation.

- The more closely training imitates the actual job environment and is participatory in style, the more effective it will be. Live scenarios can be described and assessed among the student group. That

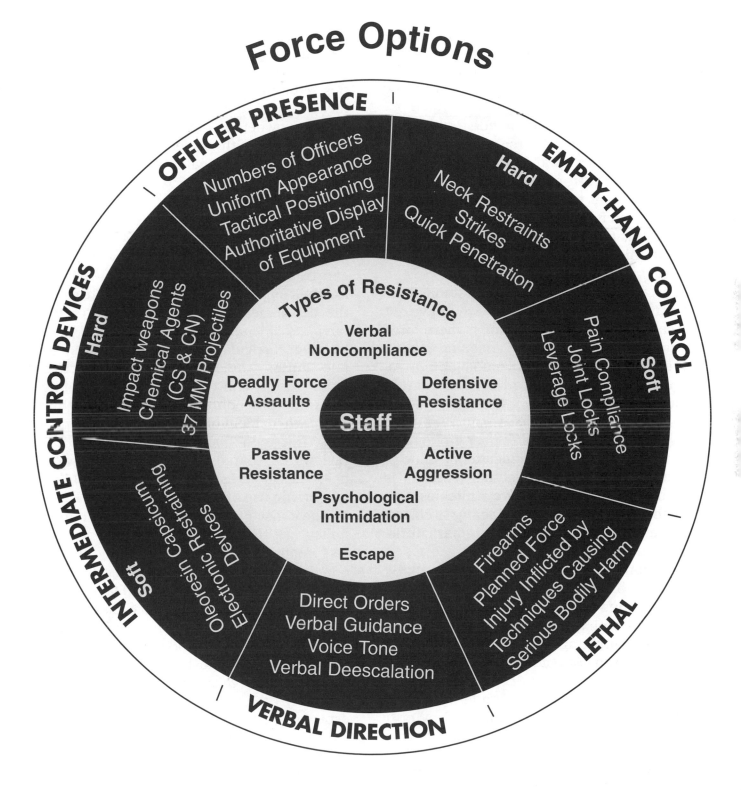

Force Options

OFFICER PRESENCE
Numbers of Officers
Uniform Appearance
Tactical Positioning
Authoritative Display
of Equipment

EMPTY-HAND CONTROL
Hard
Neck Restraints
Strikes
Quick Penetration

Soft
Pain Compliance
Joint Locks
Leverage Locks

INTERMEDIATE CONTROL DEVICES
Hard
Impact weapons
Chemical Agents
(CS & CN)
37 MM Projectiles

Soft
Oleoresin Capsicum
Oleoresin Restraining
Electronic Devices

Types of Resistance
Verbal
Noncompliance
Deadly Force
Assaults
Defensive
Resistance
Staff
Passive
Resistance
Active
Aggression
Psychological
Intimidation
Escape

LETHAL
Firearms
Planned Force
Injury Inflicted by
Techniques Causing
Serious Bodily Harm

VERBAL DIRECTION
Direct Orders
Verbal Guidance
Voice Tone
Verbal Deescalation

81

process could be enhanced by using video presentations of live or staged events with subsequent discussion and evaluations. Lethal force teams can be trained with shoot, don't shoot videos, or with building clearing or hostage extractions staged in actual buildings. Empty-handed restraint is best trained with live demonstrations using protective gear. These are just a few of the ways to bring reality to the classroom.

- Force training should include the concept that applications of force can never occur in a vacuum and are strongly related to ongoing relations with inmates. Use of force should never be considered as separate and unrelated to the techniques for deescalating an angry, volatile situation with inmates before use of force becomes necessary.

- Force training should provide some direction and coaching for those who have not experienced tense situations where force may be required. Some coaching related to the importance of overcoming normal fears and adrenaline flows to remain focused is important for all staff.

- The significance of informal training through supervisory and peer group mentoring, including the educational value of after-action analysis of actual incidents, is important. Often, effective strategies vary depending on the local facility architecture and inmate population characteristics in the supermax climate.

- A minimum level of use-of-force skills must be assured for each student who completes the training. This standard should be expressed in terms of proficiency in the use of equipment in live testing scenarios and comprehension displayed in written and oral testing.

- Staff must be trained to understand that the code of silence is prohibited by policy. The law requires that all involved in and witnesses to uses of force provide a detailed, written report before leaving duty. Administrators must stress that failure to report will be treated as willful, unprofessional conduct worthy of severe discipline or dismissal.

Policy

With the tremendous growth and expansion in corrections in the last two decades, correctional agencies, for the most part, have become large organizations. As such, they cannot afford to operate a collection of facilities as though each were an independent element with freedom of decision making on all issues. Nowhere is that condition more compelling than with issues related to use of force. The most critical tool in a standardized approach is policy.

Policy is the cornerstone of all use-of-force programs. Given the unique character of supermax prisons, policy takes on a higher level of significance. Indeed, many of the staff and trainers at those facilities are relied on for their experience and expertise to advise the department on issues related to use of force. Policy should shape attitude, drive training curricula, describe processes, outline duties and performance objectives, define terms, and describe reporting obligations and procedures. Policy should require that each incident of use of force be debriefed and the conclusions of administrative reviews be shared with staff. Policy should make a clear and strong statement of philosophy on the use of force.

The consequences of staff failing to follow policy are that they become confused and less confident about doing their jobs. Such confusion often leads to poor decision making, poor outcomes in court, and failure of the organization to meet its facility mission.

With the ingredients of a use-of-force policy in mind, successful policy development is an art. Policy should be comprehensive but not too restrictive and recognize the need for flexibility based on a variety of conditions—especially that the factors involved in each use-of-force incident may be significantly different than others. Policy should be reviewed frequently and, as a result, reflect guidance on current issues. Lastly, the value of policy is significantly reduced without a companion system for determining compliance and quality of performance. Most quality correctional systems have an entire program to determine policy compliance and provide constructive support towards improvement in such areas as security. This program complements the administrative oversight and normally includes a section on use of force.

Documentation

Use-of-force programs in supermax facilities cannot succeed without documentation. The saying that if it is not documented, it did not happen is important in these situations. Failure to document seriously weakens the credibility of staff when they are involved in judicial review. It also impairs staff's ability to accurately reconstruct events when they are called upon to do so.

All uses of force must be documented thoroughly by all involved whether as participants or witnesses. The information provided forms a database that comprises the complete historical record of each use-of-force event. All officers should be required to complete an incident report covering the basics of who, what, where, and when before they leave the end of the shift. That information, along with a medical examination report, photographs, and videotapes, should be attached to a standardized, consolidated report form which is routed up the chain of command.

The reporting form should include critical information such as: the identity of the inmate; the reason for the use of force; whether a medical exam has been completed; a description of the inmate's behavior; the amount and type of force used; and the names of staff and inmate witnesses. In relation to the administrative oversight process, the administrative head of the facility must declare *in writing* whether the force used was appropriate considering the factors surrounding the event. The need for this type of declaration says to the world that we assume full responsibility for our conduct in each use of force. The amount of documentation may seem excessive to some staff. Jurisdictions operating a supermax system, however, will

not survive judicial review without a thorough history of documentation on each use-of-force incident and major decision with respect to managing inmates. It is a lot of work with high dividends in the form of long-term survival.

Force Technology

The array of choices related to use-of-force equipment used in supermax prisons has broadened significantly in the past years. Recent trends are mostly in the direction of weapons that limit physical contact, are low impact, and, in most cases, are less than lethal in their effect. Improvements in force technology, along with serious efforts at evaluation and selection of equipment, have provided staff with the tools necessary for the job—while minimizing injury and preserving a high degree of safety for everyone.

Because correctional agencies have experienced tremendous periods of growth in the recent past, standardizing force options and related technologies has become necessary for the sake of efficiency (in terms of initial costs, effectiveness, staff training needs, and operations). All equipment selected for use should be officially approved by the department executive staff. Choices should be the product of thoughtful, long-term planning that considers factors such as reliability, proven performance, and legal history. The selection process should include the participation of correctional staff who are experienced in the use of force. Some examples of use of force technology that are currently available include the following:

- electrified perimeters
- radio communication systems for tactical convenience
- improved gas masks and riot helmets
- improved chemical weapons and delivery systems
- specialized ordnance such as flashbang, stingball rounds, and ricochet-proof ammunition

- handheld and specialized electronic control devices
- new and better types of body armor
- disabling foams
- new and better restraint devices
- infrared vision for towers and perimeter vehicles
- delivery of control chemicals by high-intensity water stream both into prison cells and over long distances

Choices of equipment are driven by staff preference, budget, and legal issues. Making such choices are not easy decisions in the face of the multitude of vendors and alternatives offered today.

Conclusion

We have described the various force options available to staff in supermax prisons. In addition to supporting administrative and training systems, we have emphasized the importance of philosophy and principles of using force and their relationship to all aspects of successful inmate management. The highest form of staff effectiveness is to use a variety of skills in gaining cooperation and compliance from inmates. Application of physical force is one of those skills and must not be separate and distinct from other aspects of relations with inmates. Professional correctional officers must be skilled communicators and problem solvers. Working with inmates in the supermax environment requires the ability to control, diffuse, and resolve tense situations, and avoid unnecessary escalation of conflict. Uses of force must be performed with confidence and professionalism and reflect a sense of duty to act, an ongoing concern for relationships with inmates, and the existence of reasonable thinking in operating the organization.

ENDNOTES

[1] Inmate Profile Data, Colorado State Penitentiary, 1993 to present.

[2] Madrid v. Gomez, 889 F.Supp. 1146, 1179 (ND Cal. 1995), page 14.15.

[3] Ibid., pages 14-15

[4] Bell v. Wolfish, 441 US 520 (1079), page 36.

[5] Madrid v. Gomez, 889 F.Supp 1146, 1179 (ND Cal. 1995), page 71.

[6] Hudson v. McMillian, 503 U.S. 1, 112 S.Ct. 995, 117 L. Ed. 2nd 156 (1992).

[7] Use Of Force Database, Colorado State Penitentiary, 1996 to present.

[8] Craig Hemmens, J.D., Ph.D., and Eugene Atherton, B.A., 1999. Use of Force: Current Policy and Practice. Lanham, Maryland: American Correctional Association, pages 56-57.

[9] Ibid., pages 48-49.

[10] Ibid., pages 48-49.

Chapter 7: Inmate Incentive Programs

James H. Bruton
Warden (retired)
Oak Park Heights Correctional Facility
Stillwater, Minnesota

Introduction

The underlying philosophy of running a maximum-security or supermax prison begins with treating offenders with dignity and respect. Administrators must set an example by treating the incarcerated like they would want their mother, father, sister, or brother treated if they were confined. Setting this type of tone throughout the facility will promote the positive environment incentive-based programming tries to create. Punishment should not be left to be carried out within the prison environment. It is to be left with the courts.

The basic premise of an incentive-based program is to develop a solid base of support for this program throughout all levels of the organization. The staff involved in the security of the program and the program civilian staff must have a positive attitude toward the goals and an enthusiasm for the program's existence. Without these critical elements, the program is doomed to failure. Programming that has a reason to exist must be developed—whether it be to prepare offenders for release or to prepare offenders to live a positive life while incarcerated.

Whether the program is education-based, recreational, therapy designed, or work related, it must have a mission and be under close scrutiny and evaluation. Offenders must understand and appreciate the importance and significance of being program participants to the point of recognizing how positive behavior has rewards and negative behavior has swift and immediate consequences.

This chapter will discuss incentive-based programming in maximum-security or supermax prisons. It will focus on the importance of setting up programs that will provide offenders with an opportunity for participation based on their behavior. The punishment for those incarcerated is being sentenced to prison and being detained in a controlled and confined setting. Corrections professionals are not responsible for continuing to punish offenders beyond the sanction of incarceration. This philosophy must be established along with the awareness that the majority of offenders who come to prison will eventually be released. Only then can the positive nature and importance of incentive-based programming become a reality. This type of programming is a critical element of prison operations at all levels of security, especially at the higher custody levels.

Basic Philosophy of Incentive-based Programming

Once there is an understanding and acceptance that the punishment is being incarcerated and that all but a few offenders will someday be released, the foundation of incentive-based programming is established. This foundation will set a standard for everything else needed to safely operate the high-custody prison. One of the fundamental principles of the foundation relates to how offenders are treated while they are incarcerated. It is perhaps the cornerstone for all staff/offender interaction and should be of the highest priority. Offenders must be treated with dignity and respect at all times even though their behavior may warrant consequences or restrictions.

Administrators need to model their behavior, set an example, and train staff to understand the importance of this concept—because how offenders are treated will set the tone for everything else that is important in a prison's daily operations. It must be practiced at all levels of the organization from the line officer and the support staff to the highest of administrators.

In the mind of offenders, the prison environment is an extremely negative one. They are away from their families and living in a controlled setting with their freedom removed. Treating offenders with dignity and respecting them as persons is the start of their understanding that an environment exists to help them make positive changes in their lives if they choose to do so.

Staff interactions and communications with offenders should be professional, respectful, and consistent. Offenders in the controlled environment of a prison setting who are treated with dignity and respect are more likely to respond in a positive manner and have a better chance of success in programming. The reaction to positive encounters with staff, in most cases, provides offenders with the necessary stimuli to motivate them toward positive behavior.

The positive environment that is created in a supermax prison does not happen by accident or luck; it happens by design. The positive incentive-based prison environment is a carefully planned out and thoughtfully created management tool. When programs run smoothly with little problems, they do so because they are carefully designed and foundationally sound. The programs must reflect the philosophy that is expected and modeled from the top administrator; the philosophy must never be eroded. All programs must be reviewed and evaluated continuously to ensure that they remain intact and are valid.

It is the warden's ultimate responsibility to set the tone for what is expected from staff at all levels of the organization. The primary objective of a prison's operations is to create an environment that is conducive to rehabilitation for those offenders who truly want to make a change in their lives. Therefore, establishing programming incentives that encourage involvement is critical. If individuals have no desire to make a change in lifestyle, however, positive programming will have little or no effect on their behavior. These offenders will be easy to identify usually based on their attitude and behavior. Initially, these offenders may exhibit anger and determination to maintain their though-guy image. They may act out their anger by calling correctional officers or other offenders names, throwing noxious substances, or other inappropriate behaviors. They leave staff with no alternative than to place the offenders in their cells most of the day. In Minnesota, a state law requires offenders to participate in a program assignment if one is available. If they choose not to do so, they are charged with a disciplinary infraction and may be penalized by extended incarceration time. Most offenders will cooperate with programming once they learn and understand the advantages of being out of their cells and active most of the day. Even when programming is not mandated by law, and when offenders must participate in programs from their cells, the majority of offenders choose to participate in programs. This occurs for two primary reasons. First, programs provide stimulation. Second, program participation is often the path out of the facility.

A program environment that can help offenders learn how to read or do a particular job undoubtedly will lead to a positive attitude in the prison environment and have an influence on other offenders as well. It also will help them develop important life skills that may lessen their likelihood of reoffending. Finally, this type of learning hopefully will enhance offenders' self-respect and motivate them to lead a lifestyle consistent with society's expectations. Being involved in programming will help offenders discover their capabilities and enhance their self-worth. Obtaining a high school education (or developing a marketable skill) will not only help offenders develop a positive attitude but also demonstrate for others what is available to them and how a good attitude and desire can lead to achievement. The expectations of society center around individuals being good citizens, being law-abiding, and making positive contributions. Coming out of prison with some foundational support for this can be positive for offenders. What offenders have learned and experienced during their years of incarceration will be a major contributing factor toward how they adjust in the community upon release. Most people living in society will not have a choice about who is going to be their next door neighbor, who is going to live in their neighborhood, or who will sit next to them in a movie theater. If they find themselves interacting with offenders or ex-offenders, having a positive experience take place is desirable.

Society's Expectations

Sometimes, the general public appears to want it both ways. When it comes to managing offenders, society wants to see offenders punished for their crimes and to have fewer advantages or amenities than those living in the community. At the same time, however, society also may want to see the offenders rehabilitated. Both expectations cannot be accomplished, but a compromise may be reached. If we consider that the vast majority of offenders who come to prison eventually will be released, the planning and programming for them becomes clear. We must find ways to create a supportive environment for offenders who want to be rehabilitated. If offenders are allowed to develop basic life skills—earn a high school diploma or an advanced degree, or even learn how to get up every day and go to work—rehabilitation is on the right track. Society ultimately will want offenders rehabilitated because it is the best for the community as well as the offenders. Once released, these offenders have a greater opportunity to adjust in a positive, socially accepted manner.

Managing Offenders Who May Never Be Released

It may become routine practice for the legislature to pass a mandatory sentencing law; for the courts to impose a long-term sentence; or for the public to be pleased with a decision that sends an offender to prison with no opportunity for release. Many members of society may choose to believe that the matter is resolved with a guilty verdict. However, the reality is that managing the offenders becomes the responsibility of corrections professionals.

Some offenders will never be released from prison because of their sentence or the nature of their crime. Some professionals may question why these offenders are offered programming or why they should face anything but the maximum type of cell confinement of twenty-three hours a day (in most settings, a mandatory period of one hour of recreation is required). If they experience nothing but lengthy cell confinement, offenders who face a lifetime of incarceration can and do pose a serious threat to other offenders and staff. Interacting and often reacting to the behavior of the most dangerous and predatory offenders becomes a reality for staff. For example, staff will encounter the offenders during patdown (body) and cell searches. Therefore, the importance of creating a positive environment with the opportunity for change is instrumental in controlling the offenders' behavior. Incentive-based programming and rehabilitation techniques provide a positive environment and reduce the likelihood of the offenders acting out. Even for those who have established a history of violent and negative acting out, incentives and rewards for positive behavior will effectively reduce the frequency of the offenders' problem behavior—despite secure cell confinement and restrictions. Similarly, even long-term offenders will more than likely adjust positively to the opportunity to be involved in productive assignments.

Long-term offenders who have virtually nothing to lose by exhibiting negative behavior and nothing to gain by exhibiting positive behavior become a serious threat to safety and security. These offenders need something to look forward to every day, such as a visit or recreation. But the key to managing long-term offenders is giving them opportunities to be involved in productive assignments. By using the incentive-based program as a management tool, staff can create an environment that is likely to focus the offenders' mind on the positive and off the negative of a hopeless future.

Inmate idleness should be one of the biggest concerns of every prison administrator. Keeping offenders busy and their minds occupied in a positive way is important. Offenders who are incarcerated in high-security prisons in most cases have exhibited violent behavior. Therefore, what they are thinking and doing is critical. If offenders awake every morning and have a reason to get out of bed to go to work, school, or whatever it may be—even if some of the programming is offered in their own cells—the chances of their causing problems during the day is reduced. When offenders have idle time, they will have a strong tendency to act out and create problems.

The rewards that come with good behavior may vary. A reward may be a "unit night" with special privileges for those in a living unit who have worked hard in their job assignments over a period of time. A reward may be a break in the workday and donuts and coffee for completing a project or for demonstrating good behavior for a period of time. A reward may be an outside speaker in education classes or a special meal depending on the circumstances that lead to the reward. An administrator has a lot of latitude to put rewards in place.

Even for those who do not respond and have to spend most of their day in their cell, there must be incentives that will enhance their desire to behave. A reward may be something as simple as allowing offenders to have a magazine or a radio. All levels of behavior must have a reward system in place. The system works and needs constant evaluation and fine tuning tailored to each particular circumstance and individual.

Incentive-based Programs in High-security Prisons

An incentive-based program is a process in place that is conducive to the rehabilitation of offenders who are inclined to make changes in their lives. It may be a work program that develops job skills; an education program that provides for educational opportunities; or a therapy program that can help offenders work on the problems that contributed to their criminal behavior. The elements of the program are the ingredients available that exist to provide incentives for offenders to want to change and then actually make the changes. The program starts with the attitudes of the staff, the credibility of the program, and the availability to the offenders.

Programming in high-security prisons, such as a supermax, focuses on a different approach than programming in lower-security prisons. If developed properly, incentive-based programming with rewards for good behavior and immediate sanctions for negative behavior will have a major effect on the overall operation of the prison. Incentives are a key ingredient of high-security programs. However, security, control, and well-trained professional staff are equally important.

Administrators always must be aware of who the programming is designed for and recognize the problems and potentially dangerous situations that may exist for each type of program established. When they are working with offenders in high-custody prisons, staff must be aware of the offenders' potential for violent behavior and the necessity to follow security procedures.

Programming Controversy

Providing incentive-based programming in high-security prisons for offenders is a very controversial issue. The general public and many corrections professionals believe that long-term offenders and/or violent offenders are too dangerous to be out of their cells for extended periods or to receive programming. However, these offenders often set the foundation for the program and establish a support base by setting a positive example for others to follow. The length of their incarceration may determine their need for the positive incentive-based environment more than for short-term offenders.

One issue that seems to bring out the controversy is the concept of offenders serving life sentences or "lifers" getting an education in prison. The controversy centers on providing an education for offenders who may never be released from prison. In addition to creating a positive environment for the offenders to spend their time while incarcerated, another important aspect is rarely considered. This aspect is the connection that develops between the family and community to the programming and the positive effects that it may have on them.

For example, consider a particular lifer housed in the maximum-security prison at Oak Park Heights in Minnesota. He had been a problem inmate in the system for many years until he enrolled in the education program and eventually achieved an associate arts degree. He worked hard for some time to earn the degree and shortly before his transfer to a lesser custody facility, he wrote a letter to all of the other education unit offenders.

In the letter, he stated that receiving the degree was the first time in the fifty-two years of his life that his family had ever been proud of him. It was the first time that his children and grandchildren looked up to him. They said that if he could get a degree, they also could do better in school. This program option and the success that came with it were of great significance to the offender, his family, and the community.

Training Staff to Understand and Support Programming

Those providing security and working with the offenders every day must have a clear understanding of the expectations and institution philosophy about incentive-based programming. A program can easily erode from its mission if staff do not support or understand the importance of incentives toward safety and security. Staff must have the ability and understand the need to communicate with the offenders and work with them toward resolving their daily concerns. Communication with offenders should not be confused with loss of control or lack of discipline; rather, it should be a positive tool to lessen the frustrations that go with incarceration.

Well-trained and experienced staff will understand and support the need for incentive-based programming at all security and custody levels—including supermax. Through training and experience, staff will understand the importance of and need for this type of programming, and what can occur when all hope is taken away from the offender. Staff must be trained and learn that a unit, a program area, and an entire prison can become a treacherous and unsafe environment quickly. If a work area, school, classroom, or recreation area is properly staffed and rich in programming and incentives, the frequency of problems is reduced. This is why administrative on-site observation of the program areas and constant checks and balances to ensure that the established practices have not eroded is critical. The same principle holds true for in-cell programming.

If the program is meeting its goals and the staff support it, offenders will learn to understand that negative behavior may result in the loss of the positive environment. In addition, staff will learn to recognize and identify offenders who are not following expectations, and remove them from the program.

Staff will know whether the program is meeting its goals through attending meetings about evaluations and assessments of the program. However, the real report card on the success of the program is the number of incidents that occur which connect to the program. A successfully run incentive-based program will have few incidents, if any, over long periods of time.

A team approach is important to establishing staff's "ownership" of the program. Their continual participation in the day-to-day supervision and the evaluation of the program is key. In addition, staff want to be part of a program that is operating safely and effectively.

Staff at all levels of the organization must support what occurs in the positive programmed units. Therefore, the uniformed staff who are assigned to these areas must communicate with others and support their roles and responsibilities. Officers and supervisors must work closely with teachers, industry foremen and forewomen, therapists, caseworkers, and others to achieve the program goals. Once again, this principle holds true for in-cell programming.

Once the program base has been established, consistency and reinforcement of positive behavior is essential. Rewards that are in place and special recognitions will enhance the development of the program and be appreciated by staff, and by the offenders as well.

Once the staff are clear about what is expected in these areas on a daily basis, the majority of offenders likely will follow suit. When offenders understand the concepts and philosophies in place along with the rules and expectations, the positively programmed environment has been established. Offenders will know that they can be removed from this environment through negative behavior and that alone should set the tone for their future behavior. At the Colorado State Penitentiary,

inmate behavior determines privilege level. Each incentive level has well-defined benefits for compliance with expected behaviors. Negative behaviors do not meet expectations and cause the inmate to immediately regress to lower incentive levels. Even when offenders are in the lowest privilege level, there are incentives to motivate positive behaviors. In extreme cases where the offender refuses to follow directives, mental health staff develop behavioral management plans. Mental health staff must work extremely closely with correctional staff to ensure guidelines of the plan are followed. Only when the offender learns he is responsible for his behavior and that his behavior directly impacts his lifestyle will change in behavior occur.

Visiting as an Incentive

Contact visiting is an important element of an incentive-based program. It creates an opportunity for the offender to spend time with a friend or loved one in a setting more comfortable than the divided secure rooms afforded by the telephone visit. During a telephone visit, two secure rooms with a wall between them divide the parties so that they cannot have any physical contact. The contact visit does create the potential for problems to occur in the visiting room such as the introduction of contraband, offender incompatibilities, and disruptive activity. The contact visit remains important, however, because most offenders will control their behavior on a daily basis to avoid losing the opportunity for the contact visit. Facilities that do not provide the contact visiting opportunity for offenders lose a major control feature of daily operations Even in supermax facilities, where contact visiting is not allowed, incentives for proactive behavior can be developed. For example, offenders in higher privilege levels may have longer visiting hours or better visiting days.

When a prison administrator evaluates the importance of incentive-based programming, visiting will be one of the critical aspects of it. Perhaps the most important thing to offenders is their ultimate release date. If this is true, then the second most important thing is their visits with loved ones. The contact visit that is a reward for good behavior not only gives offenders and their families an opportunity for positive communication but also serves as a major contributor to the institution environment. If offenders know that negative behavior will reduce their opportunity for the contact visit, their behavior, in most cases, can be driven toward the positive. Contact visits do produce a positive environment and often drive and influence good behavior. This behavior transfers with offenders to lesser custody levels and to the community. In Minnesota prisons several years ago, administrators greatly reduced the introduction of contraband at higher-custody facilities by controlling the way contact visits were conducted. These changes are still in effect. Except for a short hug and kiss on the cheek only at the beginning and at the end of the visit, no physical contact is allowed during the visit. The offender and visitor are required to sit across from each other and refrain from any physical contact. Staffing is intense in the area, and contraband control is the highest priority of the visiting surveillance.

At the high-security prison at Oak Park Heights from 1982 to the start of this policy in 1995, staff arrested more than 100 visitors attempting to introduce contraband into the prison. From 1995 to 2002, staff have not arrested any visitors for introducing contraband. For serious violators of prison rules, noncontact visiting does remain an option. Decisions are made to restrict visits after violations are reviewed by the supervisor of the visiting area, a visiting committee, and the warden. Visiting privileges are revoked for short periods of time to permanent loss. An offender who is part of a plan to introduce contraband into a facility loses contact visits for ten years in Minnesota. The visitor is barred for life and prosecuted. The policy has worked and is supported not only by the absence of visitor arrests but also by few positive drug tests of offenders (random and suspicion testing is done frequently). In addition,

the state legislature banned all tobacco in prisons in 1998. Since that time, only one cigarette butt has been found. This result adds credibility for allowing the contact visit as an incentive for positive behavior, yet illustrates that contraband introduction during visits can be controlled significantly. At the Colorado State Penitentiary, contact visits are not allowed. However, inmates who are caught with drugs or tobacco lose their privilege to visit. Each infraction results in longer losses of the privilege.

The Role of Security in Incentive-based Programs

There is little opportunity for incentive-based programming to be successful in a high-security prison without a solid security system in place. Staff and offenders must clearly understand that security is critical to the long-term success of any program. Some correctional administrators believe that programming does not belong at this custody level because the offenders are potentially too dangerous to be out of their cells for extended periods or to be provided programming.

In this environment, the potential for problems always exists. However, if security systems are operated correctly, the frequency of incidents and the likelihood of serious disturbances can be greatly reduced. The trade off from lockdown to incentive-based programming provides the nucleus toward operating a safe, secure, and humane environment. Staff, from the line level to administrators, must be reminded constantly that most offenders will at some point be released. Therefore, a responsible method to reduce the frequency of their return should be in place. Corrections professionals at all levels of the organization must bear the responsibility of the environment that is created and know that it will have a significant effect on the behavior of offenders—in prison and in the community upon release.

Prison philosophy that endorses permanent lockdown as a method to operate a safe and secure environment does not always work. Offenders who are locked in their cells most of the day still find opportunities to assault staff during cell shakedowns and/or movement to other areas of the facility. Researchers have advised that offenders in the most secure environments spend most of their time trying to find ways to break the rules or injure staff. These offenders have nothing else to do and focus on the negative rather than the positive. Incentive-based programming operated properly does create a safe, secure and humane environment—even for those locked in their cells such as a supermax setting.

There must be a solid commitment to incentive-based programs and a belief that they do work to reduce the frequency of disturbances in the institution. The programs also may have a carryover effect of good and stabilized behavior in offenders who are released, which makes the effort worthwhile for both the offenders and the facility.

Security is essential and critical, however, in high-security institutions. No programming should ever take its place. Both must work hand-in-hand. One cannot be effective without the other. Programs will not work unless they have a component of high security. Similarly, security is enhanced by programming because it influences offenders to refrain from becoming a security problem.

Consistency in security is vital. Staff must be trained to understand and appreciate its importance and necessity. Offenders must know that security is present but not be aware of the regularity of its practice. Critical rules, regulations, and practices can never be compromised because consistency is what provides the basis for a safe operation.

Security systems must involve a variety of methods to control every aspect of programming. These methods may include but are not limited to the following:

- tool control
- repeated area shakedowns
- pat searches
- metal detection
- camera observation
- direct staff supervision

- offender interaction with uniformed supervisors and administrators

Tool Control

The type of program under consideration will determine the tool control that needs to be established. First, the facility must clearly identify the type and the parameters of the program and then decide what type of tool, if any, will be necessary and permitted. High-security programming should limit the tools available to offenders and avoid those that have the potential to be used as a weapon.

All tools or instruments that will be used by offenders must be screened for potential problems. If there is any doubt or concern, an instrument cannot be a part of the program. Program administrators should employ shadowboards, and staff need to take several daily inventories at all program locations. A solid method to control tools is to have a sign-out and sign-in method for all tools. In addition, staff should periodically check during the shift to ensure that each tool is under the control of the offender who checked it out. These types of check and balance procedures ensure that the tools are controlled and accounted for while in the possession of the offender.

Offenders should never be permitted to leave an area until all tools are accounted for and all policy and procedures connected to the check in have been completed. If a tool is missing or unaccounted for, a lockdown of the unit may be in order. Staff should follow policies and procedures to search for the missing tool.

If the process to locate the tool takes several days or up to a week, the offenders may need to remain under lockdown status. The consequences and established methods to find the tool will dictate how the unit operates on a daily basis. Any security deviation from policy most likely will have a direct influence on the impact of the lost tool incident and how it affects the program.

Tools could be lost when maintenance staff make repairs in a cell. Almost any piece of metal can be fashioned into a tool or a weapon. Most supermax cells are primarily concrete, which is a good sharpening device. Inmates are adept at locating items in a cell that can be dismantled to make a weapon. For example, one inmate managed to "cut" a shank from the back of his steel door.

Shakedowns

Unexpected and periodic unit shakedowns are essential. Routine searches of inmates and the work or program areas must be thorough and completed on a daily basis. These routine security procedures are an important aspect of daily prison operations and should be consistent with policy and procedure. These shakedowns are unexpected and involve a carefully planned-out process that may take up to a week to complete depending on the size of the living unit and program area. The searches are in contrast to the routine searches of cells and areas–searches that are a part of everyday procedures in high-security prisons.

A strategy that involves this type of security process may work successfully assuming the offenders involved in the program live in the same complex or cellblock. For discussion purposes, we will discuss how an industry program implements the process. At the completion of tool inventory on a given day and after the offenders are secured for count prior to lunch, all offenders are advised that the unit is under a routine lockdown. Each is provided with a memorandum from the unit supervisor that discusses how the lockdown will proceed and what will occur over the next several days. Simultaneously, as the unit is notified of the lockdown in progress, staff conduct entries into several suspicious cells to look for contraband. Staff must be fully trained in the cell shakedown procedures to ensure that the process is consistent with the timing of the lockdown.

Over the course of the next several days, while the unit is on lockdown status, staff carefully search each cell to look for contraband. All work areas are also searched during the lockdown period. If the lockdown is routine, administrators must decide whether telephone, visiting, exercise, and shower privileges will be permitted or denied to avoid compromising the security of the lockdown.

At the conclusion of the cell shakedowns and the program areas, the final phase includes individual interviews of all unit offenders. Even if the lockdown is purely routine and there is no suspicion of any problems, the interviews should still occur. They should be done privately and an established set of questions predetermined by supervisors should set the tone for the interviews. The ultimate goal and purpose of the interviews is to establish an update on the unit operations, and to identify the issues and concerns that may exist in the minds of the offenders— whether real or imagined. These interviews should provide staff and administrators with an overall analysis on how the unit is functioning. Administrators and staff should be able to assess whether there is tension in the unit and identify the positive or negative attitudes of the offenders that may influence the unit operations in the future.

Unannounced lockdowns should occur several times a year. The same process with some variations should also occur during a nonroutine lockdown. This type of lockdown could occur after an incident in the unit or program area or after a tool is missing. Procedures during this type of lockdown may focus on the incident specifically or may fall into the established procedure of the routine lockdown. Administrators must make other security decisions during the lockdown. For example, if the lockdown is routine, offenders may be able to have visiting, exercise, use the phone, and take showers. However, during the nonroutine lockdown, administrators must assess the seriousness of the incident to determine whether privileges will be suspended. The lockdown is a timeout period from routine daily activity and a report card check of what the status of the unit is at the given time.

Pat Searches, Cameras, and Metal Detectors

Any area of a high-security prison where offenders live, work, attend school or engage in other types of activity must have metal detectors and must use pat searches for offender entrance and departure to and from the area. Because the highest priority must be the safety of staff and offenders, pat searches of the offenders are essential.

Few security procedures are more critical than the pat search; yet, it is perhaps the procedure most often done incorrectly. This is because staff conduct pat searches so often and rarely find contraband. Staff need to be continually advised about the importance of conducting proper pat searches and trained on the proper way to conduct them.

In high-security prisons, homemade weapons can become routinely available if security systems are not in place and effective. One of the best security devices is the video camera. These cameras should be placed in strategic locations so that program areas are under constant surveillance. The camera can become an effective deterrent to negative behavior and also can provide valuable evidence of an incident that may have occurred in the area.

Metal detectors are expensive but also necessary. Every staff member and all offenders must know that when they depart from an area, they will move through a metal detector. When they enter another area, they again will pass through a metal detector. Although some weapons can pass metal detection, such as plastic and glass, metal detectors are a huge deterrent and an important check for weapons. In a supermax facility, it is essential to remove every item in the cell for inspection by a fluoroscope. In this manner, the needle in the haystack is most likely to be located.

The key ingredient to any incentive-based program is its safety and longevity. The program will last, the incentives will be there, and as a result the prison will operate more safely if security systems are in place and used properly.

Staff-Offender Interaction

All of the security systems established will not totally prevent the potential for serious incidents and disturbances in a high-security prison. The high-security environment houses individuals who generally have histories of settling their problems with violence. Therefore, an important management tool, and one that usually has an effect even greater than the camera and metal detector, is the direct supervision of the program. In fact, the pat search, metal detector, and camera will provide detection; however, regular staff interaction with offenders may be more of a deterrent than any other method.

Regular staff-offender interaction helps minimize offender issues, whether they are real or imagined. Those incarcerated in high-security environments are prone to settle their problems and issues by violent means. By having regular communication with staff, problems rarely rise to the level of frustration that develops into incidents or disturbances.

Staff at all levels of the organization must regularly interact with the offenders. If the issues, problems, concerns, and daily difficulties are addressed and there is not frustration due to unresolved issues, the efficiency of the program and, most important, the safety of everyone will increase. Wardens and high-level administrators are included in this interaction. They must be in the areas routinely interacting with staff and offenders. This practice will "communicate" that the unit and program are important and safety is a high priority. Administrative interaction does not take the place of staff responsibility but, instead, demonstrates support of the program and an awareness of its goals. Offenders confined in a supermax environment have limited communication ability. When the administration walks and talks to offenders, it gives the offenders an opportunity to be heard. Additionally, walking and talking to the offenders gives administrative staff a feel for the facility, sometimes allowing them to act before a problem exists.

Incidents/Disturbances in Incentive-based Programs

Minor or major incidents in program areas of high-security prisons may have a significant damaging affect on the program, the offenders who are in the program, and the staff who supervise the program. Therefore, careful follow up and planning must take place after an incident to ensure that future decisions are based on thorough assessment and solid information.

In 1999, a serious staff assault occurred at the maximum-security prison at Oak Park Heights in the industry shop. It occurred on a Friday afternoon when an offender left his work site, went to another work area, and took control of a large wrench. He proceeded across the complex and violently assaulted one of the unit foremen. During the unprovoked attack, he struck the foreman several times in the head, causing severe injury. The assault could have been worse if another offender had not intervened by creating a diversion that brought the attacker to him and caused him to be stabbed several times with a screwdriver. The incident was extremely violent, and each victim was seriously injured.

Immediately after the incident, the unit was secured and placed on lockdown status. All of the offenders in the area of the incident cooperated fully in following direct orders and switching into their cells. As the investigation continued over the next several hours and into Saturday morning, administrators decided by noon on Saturday that the unit would reopen. The offenders in the unit would enter routine weekend programming. Some staff became immediately concerned because they believed that the unit should remain in lockdown because it was too early to reopen the unit. During the follow up after the incident, administrators determined that all fifty-one of the offenders other than the attacker followed orders. Each of these offenders was interviewed individually three separate times over the course of the evening and the following morning. Administrators determined from the evidence, intelligence gathering, and offender interviews that the assault was an isolated incident, and there was no reason to keep the unit secured. Continuing the lockdown would have punished those offenders who cooperated during the incident.

The reaction of offenders who are not initially involved in an incident needs to be carefully evaluated. In the previous incident, if some offenders had switched in slowly, showed uncooperative attitudes, or provided assistance to the assault, the incident assessment may have had a different outcome. The unit may have gone into lockdown status, and shakedown procedures may have been followed. Frequently, in the supermax setting, several offenders will follow the lead of another offender acting out in a domino effect. In these cases, it is important to deal with each offender one at a time in a manner that is consistent from one individual to the other, until the incident is contained. The decisions in the aftermath of a major incident will be carefully evaluated and scrutinized by staff at all levels of the organization. Offenders also will be waiting to see how the incident is going to be handled. Therefore, these decisions are critical to the future operations of the prison and the incentive-based programming. Careful evaluation and decisions based on good information will provide support for the action taken.

Most details of incidents are not always shared, but they must be evaluated. They must be learning experiences that can help administrators tweak the program or provide a major change to reduce the frequency of a reoccurrence. Staff should be involved in postevaluations of the incidents and debriefing sessions, when appropriate.

Consequences and Rewards

The success of any incentive-based program in a high-security environment must be built on a fundamental philosophy of incentives that deliver rewards for positive behavior and swift and immediate consequences for negative behavior. If used correctly, this philosophy will cement the foundation of any successful program.

Staff should intervene immediately when negative behavior occurs. The results may vary depending on the severity of the violation. It may require a warning, room restriction for further evaluation, or movement immediately to confinement in the segregation unit. Except for the last determination, each of the initial decisions may lead to the expulsion from the program. The latter scenario is likely to lead to expulsion. In a supermax setting, the correctional staff must have the capability of implementing incentive level changes. In this manner, negative behaviors have an immediate consequence. Consequences of both negative and positive behaviors are more closely linked to create change.

If offenders are to be removed from the program, they must understand the reasons for the action. They should be moved out of the unit to another unit where positive behavior for an extended period of time will be the only avenue for return to the program. This sanction supports the concept of consequences for negative behavior and allows the offenders to exhibit positive behavior to bring the program option back to their daily routine.

Usually, removal from the program will be handled by the program supervisor who is either a civilian or uniformed staff member. The incident should be reviewed up the chain of command with the ultimate review by the warden.

For the positively acting and programmed offenders, the rewards come with the potential of:

- a future transfer to a less-secure facility
- the ability to remain out of their cell in programming for long periods of time
- day-to-day recognition that good behavior makes living in the prison environment less confining than for those who have demonstrated that they cannot be trusted in such an environment

Making the Prison Safer

Every warden who has ever had the responsibility of running a prison knows that the potential of staff injury is of utmost concern. Reviews of incidents, policy and procedure, and almost daily analysis of overall operations are always a high priority. The daily agenda should include considerations and discussions on how to lessen the frequency of incidents and how to develop new plans and procedures to make the environment a safer place in which to work and live.

The incentive-based program in a high-security prison will make the overall operations of the prison safer. However, this does not happen by accident; it happens by design. If the philosophy and goals of the programming are in place and checked on a regular basis, the program has a high probability of being successful and instrumental as a contributor to a safe environment.

Security implications talked about in this chapter are essential and will be a factor in the success of the program. In addition, continuing to evaluate the program and the atmosphere that it is creating in the prison is of the utmost importance. Offenders must have something to look forward to every day and understand that positive behavior will result in positive rewards. Offenders also must understand that negative behavior will keep them from the rewards.

History has shown that many disturbing incidents involve offenders with long sentences who have nothing to do during the day and nothing to look forward to in the future. The accounts of the events usually involve offenders who have focused their attention on everything negative. After a while, their full focus is on staff, the institution, the corrections department, and their attempt to get even for everything from their perspective that has been done wrong to them. They get up every morning with a bad attitude that is full of negativity toward everything that they encounter during the day. Offenders with such an attitude heighten the potential of incidents occurring.

When this kind of environment is created and the attitude of the offender is allowed to focus in this negative direction, the prison environment is in serious trouble. When the prison's daily operations give the message of little hope and little to look forward to in the future, major problems exist, and the frequency of incidents are likely to increase. The negative environment that is created needs to be recognized in its early stages.

Staff need to be constantly aware of the surroundings and the behavior of the offenders. The behavior of offenders sometimes will key staff into problems that are occurring or about to occur. For example, some of the friendlier offenders may become less friendly. The general tone of discussions in the unit might have diminished. Some offenders may be louder or quieter. There may be an unusual "feeling" in an area or unit. Basically, there is something different from the normal environment. All staff must observe the dynamics of the unit on their shift. The tone, intensity, and general atmosphere of the unit must be reported in writing by every shift every day. Because behavioral nuances are so important in a supermax facility, staff should maintain a log on each offender. These logs should be reviewed daily so that staff are aware of what has occurred on other shifts and can respond to any issues on their shift in a consistent manner.

A positive prison environment uses methods that put the focus on a positive and not a negative environment. Consistent assessment should be routine to insure its direction. It is the warden's or administrator's responsibility to ensure that a negative environment does not develop. If it does, the negative consequences can be dramatic. In contrast, ensuring a positive environment helps prepare offenders for rehabilitation. When this environment is established and closely monitored with the methods and philosophy illustrated in this chapter, the prison environment will help reduce the risks of working and living in the high-security prison.

Summary

The overall importance of incentive-based programming in supermax prisons cannot be overstated. It is a critical element of the day-to-day operations that will provide an avenue of hope for the offenders and will, if properly operated, reduce the frequency of incidents.

When the most dangerous and high-risk offenders are confined with no incentives in place to recognize and support positive behavior, this creates surroundings that will directly influence the safety and security of the prison. The important and realistic approach to managing the most difficult of all offenders is to program through incentives. The central idea of incentive-based programming is the philosophy of controlling the offenders in a humane and dignified manner.

At the high-security prison at Oak Park Heights in Minnesota, offenders move to programming areas in groups no larger than seven at a time. This intense form of controlled movement reduces the frequency of incidents occurring and gives the facility the confidence of generally being able to control any problems that might occur during movement. At the same time, however, the movement is completed in a dignified manner and preserves the opportunity for offenders to move to an area where programming is in place that produces positive results. Programming may include events in visiting areas, the gymnasium, the chapel, industry shops, or education classrooms.

This chapter has focused on key ingredients to programming with incentives and control of the offenders. One will not be successful without the other. Staff should be trained in both areas, including the philosophical foundation of the program and the expectations that go with it.

The type of program that is put in place for the offenders does not matter; what matters is how it operates, how it is continually evaluated, and how it is supported by staff at all levels of the organization. The issues that must be addressed and the critical elements that must be in place have been discussed in this chapter. Although there may be a wide range of program possibilities set up in the high security prison setting, the basics always will be the same. Incentive-based behavior will contribute to the well being for all staff and offenders when the foundation for it is set and the expectations are clearly defined and followed.

Some of the highlights of this type of programming are as follows:

- Treat offenders with respect and dignity.
- The punishment is being in prison. It is not the responsibility of the corrections professional to continue to administer punishment.
- Create an environment that is conducive to rehabilitation for offenders who want to make a change in their lives.
- Control and security of the program are critical elements.
- Positive behavior will receive positive rewards and negative behavior will receive swift and immediate consequences.
- The environment must be created to give offenders a reason to get out of bed every morning and to look forward to something positive in the day ahead.
- The policy and procedure for the program must be in place and it must be followed.
- Staff at all levels of the organization must understand and support the foundational approach to the program and be fully trained on the expectations for the program's success.

The prison that operates every day with a mission to provide a safe, secure, and humane environment will have a mission that includes the elements of this chapter. Staff will recognize how this incentive-based programming will heighten the importance of everything else that is done in the prison throughout all of its daily operations.

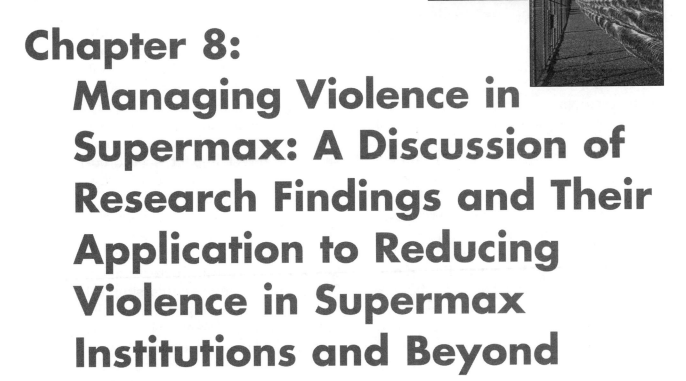

Chapter 8:
Managing Violence in Supermax: A Discussion of Research Findings and Their Application to Reducing Violence in Supermax Institutions and Beyond

Jerald Justice, MA/MSW
    Program Consultant
    California Department of Mental Health
    Vacaville, California

Myla H. Young, Ph.D., ABPN
    Senior Supervising Psychologist/Program Consultant
    California Department of Mental Health
    Vacaville, California

In this chapter, we discuss violence in society and violence in prison. We describe inmates in a supermax facility with a primary focus on the problem of violence. Then, we describe a California mental health program and the results of research within that program. Using information from this research, we provide a description of inmates referred for psychiatric treatment from both a general prison population and a prison supermax population. Based on this research information, we suggest program development ideas and interventions. We conclude the chapter with a discussion of implications of this research for managing violent inmates in a supermax facility.[1]

Violence in Society

Violence is a problem as old as humankind. Its primordial origins served to proliferate the species, and humans today carry the vestiges of this ingrained propensity for violence as a fundamental adaptive trait. Social order eventually replaced violence as the quintessential human adaptation. As society evolved, the value of violent behavior became less significant, and ultimately counterproductive. Nevertheless, violence has endured, and society has yet to develop a system of social order capable of eradicating violence among it members. Relative to most comparable countries, the United States has been disproportionately plagued with the problems associated with violence. The National Commission on the Causes and Prevention of Violence (1969) referred to the United States as "the clear leader among modern, stable, democratic nations in its rates of homicide, assault, rape, and robbery." While this report raised concern in the 1960s, the decades that followed showed progressively higher rates of violent crime across all major categories. Scientific and editorial inquiries as to the causes of this phenomena accompanied the rising crime statistics, spurring seemingly endless debate as to solutions. Many contributing and even causal factors have been identified. Understanding causation, however, while usually a prerequisite to resolving a problem, is seldom a solution in itself.

Societal tolerance for persistently increasing rates of violent crime ended abruptly in the 1990s with a plethora of federal and state legislative actions that stiffened penalties, increased sentences, and limited opportunities for parole. The enactment of California's "three strikes" legislation epitomized the intent of these new laws, which was to keep serious offenders out of society for longer periods of time. Half the states and the federal government implemented similar laws with the same intent. As a result, the correctional institution population, which had been growing steadily since the middle 1970s, would be further impacted with more inmates serving longer sentences. The concern was that prison crowding, already a major problem for some states, would reach critical proportions. To keep pace, prison construction skyrocketed. By the year 2000, there were four times the number of prison cells as compared to the 1960s. Even so, in 2000, state prisons were operating between 1 and 17 percent above capacity (Bureau of Justice Statistics, 2000). There is considerable debate as to whether this societal response will have the desired effect. Called "draconian" by some, "appropriate and overdue" by others, arguments on both sides are vehement. There is a correlation with the decrease in violent crime noted in the middle to late 1990s, yet many claim that increased incarceration accounts for only a small part of that decrease. While the ultimate societal effect remains to be seen, the direct impact on the correctional system is current, and undoubtedly, a harbinger for the foreseeable future.

The severity of violence seen in society does not abate with sentencing. With few exceptions, violence continues in prison. Evans (1996) of the Correctional Service of Canada made note of this simple but often neglected fact, stating, "Prisons clearly have not eradicated violent behavior. They have simply displaced violent activity to another time and place." As the frequency and intensity of violence increases in society, the problem is mirrored and concentrated in prisons. It is this very concentration that typifies the problem.

Violence in Prison

The majority of prisons in the United States house violent offenders, which is in accordance with their intended purpose. As in society, however, violence in prison is a problem of both prevalence and severity. Even in a violent population, as may be found in almost any state prison, a number of individuals represent the extreme high end of the violence curve. Any appreciable number of these inmates threatens even the highly regulated social order of prison. So, while incarceration effectively ensures public safety by removing the offenders from the community, the problem must be addressed within the institution, and in too many cases, again when the offender is released to society.

Traditional maximum-custody facilities and programs have become insufficient to address the scope of this problem, which is the primary reason for the emergence and the existence of the supermax concept. Specialized high-security prisons are not new. Institutions such as Alcatraz, having become in itself a social icon, will long symbolize the need to recognize and control the most difficult prisoners. Still, what is required today far exceeds what met the standard more than a half century ago. New or modified facilities designed to address the current problem constitute a new standard in security. While the term supermax is increasingly used to identify the facilities as well as the concept, it has not gained universal acceptance. There is considerable variation across the United States as to a precise definition of a supermax facility, though one characteristic is consistent. All correctional systems have tried to devote or develop specialized facilities that have, as their major purpose, the management of extremely violent inmates.

The violent propensities of the identified supermax inmate population can be appreciated to some extent by considering the proportion of the prison population determined to require supermax custody. A survey of correctional institutions across the United States and Canada (U.S. Department of Justice, 1997) looked at the relative proportion of systemwide capacity needed for supermax custody. Analyzed by institution in each state, the mean was 2.8 percent (median = 2; range = 1 – 20). Supermax facilities are, by definition and purpose, intended to house the most violent inmates in the correctional system. Using this data, this means that less than 3 percent of the inmates are determined to be in this most violent category.

Extreme dangerousness is the reason for supermax facilities, and it is also their greatest management challenge. Addressing this challenge requires a comprehensive approach. The level of security and control required for managing such a population has taken precedence in the design and implementation of the supermax concept. Invariably, plans begin with attention to structure. The physical environment must be designed or modified to provide higher levels of observation and control. Beyond architecture, however, programs and policies must reflect the major goals of safety and control.

Currently, the role of programming tends to be an adjunct to security, with the emphasis on maintaining external control rather than on producing remedial change in prisoners per se. This tendency raises a critical issue about the role of incarceration, particularly with regard to supermax facilities. There is a high degree of consensual agreement between correctional departments that the paramount goal of the correctional system is public safety. The logic in this goal is irrefutable as long as the offender is incarcerated. To that end, the recent laws that have been enacted to increase sentences, lengthen terms, and provide for continued incarceration beyond the sentence for some high-risk inmates do contribute to public safety. However, many offenders will return to society, and sooner rather than later. Beck (2000) reported that of the 585,400 inmates projected to be released from prison in 2000, 62 percent would be arrested again, and 42 percent would be sent back to jail or prison. A significant proportion of those may be expected to offend violently. This prediction accentuates an inherent fallacy in the popular public safety philosophy. Safety is ensured only to the extent that the offender is incarcerated. Once returned to society, the potential for further harm returns and may be exacerbated.

We have now reached a critical point in this discussion, that being the problems of institutional and public safety. These issues need not be viewed as mutually exclusive. The fact that most inmates, including those in supermax, will return to society cannot be ignored. With few exceptions, the most violent inmates, the 3 percent concentration housed in supermax facilities, were also the most dangerous individuals in society. There is every reason to believe that many of them will resume their violence in society upon release. This concern is further aggravated because substantial numbers of inmates are released into the community directly from supermax facilities (U.S. Department of Justice, 1997).

Any discussion of prison programs aimed at producing enduring changes in inmates must inevitably lead to the concept of rehabilitation, which is a sordid term in some circles. The concept of rehabilitation in corrections has a long and varied history in the United States. During the first half of the twentieth century, it was generally accepted, albeit in varying degrees across state correctional departments, that rehabilitation was at least a secondary goal of incarceration. Some type of rehabilitative program was identified as a major component in most prisons in the country. Even so, the idea of rehabilitation in corrections has probably always been compromised by disharmony. One faction eschews the concept in favor of punishment, and the other is committed to the belief that criminals can be changed for the better. Arguments against rehabilitation were based on the idea of "just consequences" for criminal behavior, and further augmented by a dearth of empirical evidence supporting the effectiveness of rehabilitation.

The rehabilitation detractors clearly gained the upper hand in the mid 1970s based, in no small part, on the support of a number of scientific studies that found few or no positive effects resulting from rehabilitative approaches. The most noteworthy of these was popularized by Martinson who researched an array of studies to look at treatment effectiveness (Lipton, Martinson, and Wilks, 1975). His results were summarized in the famous words "nothing works," which set the direction of correctional philosophy from then to now. Martinson's proclamation that the many studies reviewed showed rehabilitation efforts producing no appreciable effect one way or another came to be viewed as the "final analysis" or the last word on the subject. This shortsighted perspective resulted in proponents of rehabilitation not being taken seriously by administrators and legislators and being viewed as hopelessly out of touch with the evidence.

That the Martinson study was overvalued and inappropriately generalized does not derogate its conclusions. However, a closer examination of the studies used does indicate that the results were not as clear as first thought. Some studies were flawed by validity concerns and other methodological problems. Some studies evaluated programs that were actually based more on rhetoric than substance. The majority of the programs studied, though, did represent valid attempts at remediation, and a few of them did demonstrate success in meeting their goals. Most did not, and many simply failed on their own merits. The most important consideration now, however, is that Martinson's meta-analysis (analysis of research findings) was based on studies that represented the current status of rehabilitative efforts in corrections in the 1960s and 1970s. Therefore, his analysis reflects an understanding of correctional treatment that is quite dated.

A wave of new research findings has been accumulating since about the mid 1980s, and many provide valid and reliable evidence supporting treatment in prison. These programs go beyond vocational training and education, and generally incorporate some type of psychotherapeutic approach aimed at producing significant and enduring positive change. To fully appreciate the scope of the literature in this area, we refer you to the research of Gendreau (1996), Gendreau et al. (1995), and Andrews and Bonta (1994). Studies such as these offer valuable contributions to the correctional field.

The benefits of making use of these empirical investigations in corrections are threefold. First, there is convincing evidence that some interventions do, in fact, work. Secondly, consistent commonalties and characteristics of various interventions are identified, which is indicative of what can work, and what most likely will fail. Lastly, we believe that developing highly effective interventions, based on valid research and aimed at reducing recidivism, need not compromise security and safety within the supermax institution. We acknowledge that the purpose of these institutions is safety and control. The research literature is useful in developing ways to integrate treatment interventions, which may have the benefit of reducing post release violence, into the day-to-day operation of the institution.

Many of these may be minor, even subtle. Some require more deliberate and planned implementation. Ultimately, their value is in offering options for administrators of supermax facilities in designing and managing institutional programs. This will be addressed later in the chapter. Now, however, more discussion is warranted about the characteristics of violent behavior, as demonstrated in prison, and particularly in supermax prisons.

Description of Inmates in Prison and in Supermax Facilities

Assuming that public safety issues can be addressed concurrently with institutional safety, the first step in developing programs or approaches with this emphasis is to understand characteristics of the inmate population. This section provides empirical findings that describe the characteristics of an inmate population. Although data from this project describes inmates who are in prison psychiatric treatment, these inmates come from—and return to—the general prison population. We believe that the information, therefore, reasonably applies to the general prison population.

The California Psychiatric Program. One California psychiatric program (California Psychiatric Program) provides both acute and subacute psychiatric treatment to male inmates throughout the state of California. Any inmate in the California Department of Corrections who is in need of psychiatric services can be referred to this program. Inmates are admitted to the acute program for stabilization, evaluation, and short-term treatment. There are 150 acute psychiatric beds. All beds are single cells. Inmates from

all classification levels can be referred to this unit. There also are ninety subacute psychiatric beds. Inmates in this subacute program are housed in a dormitory, with fifteen inmates per dormitory.

The Research Project. To better understand the population that they were serving, in 1994 a research project at the California Psychiatric Program was initiated, and the project continues. In this project, inmates are randomly selected and provide informed consent to participate in the project. If consent is provided, the inmate is administered a comprehensive evaluation. Correctional and medical records are reviewed. A semistructured interview obtaining information about the inmate's medical, family, school, developmental, work, drug, juvenile and adult criminal, and prison adjustment histories is conducted. A comprehensive neuropsychological evaluation that includes measures of intellectual, academic, motor, attention and concentration, memory and learning, language, psychomotor, and executive functioning is completed. A comprehensive emotional evaluation that includes a mental status examination, Rorschach test, Minnesota Multiphasic Personality Inventory (MMPI2), and Psychopathy Checklist (PCL-R) is completed. Currently, 250 inmates have participated in the research.

Information from this research has been used to gain a better understanding of the inmates who are being served and for treatment planning. Projects, among others, have included developing core treatment interventions; developing treatment outcome measures; identifying risk factors for restraint and seclusion and risk factors for recidivism; understanding the impact of head injury on functioning; understanding cultural/ethnic differences in functioning; and understanding the neuropsychological functioning of inmates. Projects also have identified risk factors for violence in the community, in prison, and in prison psychiatric treatment, as well as risk factors for self-harm.

Description of Inmates in Program

Inmates throughout the state of California—including inmates from what would be described as a supermax prison—are referred to this program for treatment. We will describe the inmates (entire sample), with particular emphasis on describing characteristics of inmates who were referred from a supermax facility.

Sociodemographic Characteristics. One of the first pieces of information that we discovered was that inmates in this sample are obviously somewhat "different" from most other groups of men. Inmates in this study are generally young (average age is thirty-two years), poorly educated (average education is tenth grade), and from the lowest socioeconomic (SES) group (Myers and Bean, 1968). Caucasian not of Latino origin (40 percent) makes up the largest group, followed by African-Americans (33 percent), and Latinos (21 percent). Drug use is predominant among these inmates. Most (89 percent) report drug abuse histories. Of those abusing drugs, the majority (78 percent) are polysubstance abusers. Alcohol and/or marijuana are the drugs most frequently used first (70 percent), most (55 percent), and preferred (49 percent). Although about one-quarter of the inmates in this sample used drugs other than alcohol, marijuana, and/or inhalants, the other drugs they used were amphetamines, hallucinogens, PCP, cocaine, and others.

Violence Characteristics. These inmates are predominantly violent. Each offense for which the inmate had been convicted was ranked on a violence rating scale ranging from nonviolent offenses (prostitution, theft, drug offenses, and so forth) to violent offenses (physical assault, murder, murder with special circumstances). Using the criteria of two or more offenses that involved assault on another individual (Level 5), or murder (Level 6), or murder with special circumstances (Level 7), 57 percent of the inmates in this sample were classified as exhibiting "high violence." Twenty-six percent had murder offenses, and 49 percent had offenses that

involved assault of another individual. Twenty-six percent had life or life without parole sentences. Most of the inmates started their criminal offenses at an early age. Seventy three percent of this sample had a history of juvenile arrest, and 48 percent had a history of placement with the California Youth Authority. Age at first offense ranged from as young as seven years to as old as forty-eight years. Measures that were significantly different for inmates who were violent in the community, as compared to inmates who were not violent in the community, were identified as follows:

- 6.7 times more likely to be psychopathic
- 5 times more likely to experience illogical thoughts
- 4.1 times more likely to be married while in prison
- 3.2 times more likely to have overall neuropsychological impairment
- 2.3 times more likely to demonstrate emotional immaturity
- 2.3 times more likely to be psychotic

Another piece of information that we discovered was that violent inmates continued to be violent once they were in prison. The disciplinary offenses for each inmate were recorded. Disciplinary offenses were divided into administrative (offenses which did not involve physical harm) and serious (offenses which did involved physical harm). The average length of time in prison at the time of participation in the study was 6.9 years. During their incarceration, inmates earned an average of seven administrative prison offenses, four serious prison offenses, and a total of eleven disciplinary actions during their six-to-seven year incarceration. Considering that 26 percent of this sample had a life sentence, and the average age was thirty-two years old, if past history predicts future history, prison maladjustment is something that cannot be ignored. Risk factors for violence in prison were as follows:

- 8.3 times more likely to have a lifestyle characterized by:
  - a pattern of "blaming others" for their difficulties
  - a history of "hot headedness" and temper tantrums
  - absence of affective response
  - behavior problems in elementary school
  - a history of animal cruelty, "trashing" homes, and degrading peers
  - lack of remorse for victims
- 4.6 times more likely to report inhalant use
- 3 times more likely to have been placed in the Youth Authority
- 2.9 times more likely to be diagnosed with borderline personality disorder
- 2.7 times more likely to report a neurological injury
- 2.4 times more likely to demonstrate impaired memory and learning
- 2.1 times more likely to demonstrate overall brain impairment

Brain Functioning. Another piece of information that was gained from this project was knowledge about the brain functioning of this group of inmates. Inmates in this population reported histories of child abuse (41 percent), poor school experience (60 percent), and limited work histories (81 percent report their highest work position in the two lowest classifications; the average longest length of time at any one job was twenty-two months; 69 percent report the longest work length as less than one year). Again, a remarkably high number of these inmates also reported histories of drug abuse (89 percent), polysubstance abuse (78 percent) and—particularly destructive to developing brains—inhalant use (19 percent). Drugs were used at an early age (average age at first drug use was twelve years), and generally were persistently used throughout their lives. And, this group of men has a pervasive incidence of head injury with loss of consciousness (65 percent). Head injury was from a variety of sources, ranging from childhood seizure disorder, to traumatic head injury, to repeated "blackouts" from

drug abuse. Although finding neuropsychological impairment suggesting compromised brain functioning is not surprising, the pervasiveness of brain damage was unexpected.

The average intellectual functioning of this sample was in the Low Average Range (average IQ was 83), and the average reading ability was at the tenth grade level (range was second grade to post high school). Using an index that combines those neuropsychological tests which are most sensitive to identifying brain damage (Halstead-Reitan Impairment Index), 84 percent of the inmates were in the impaired range.

Approximately half (50 percent) were impaired across tests of attention and concentration; more than half (54 percent) were impaired on tests of memory and learning; and almost three-quarters (73 percent) were impaired on tests of executive functioning. Executive functioning is the ability to think, reason, problem solve, maintain impulse control, anticipate the consequences of your actions BEFORE acting, change ineffective behaviors to effective behaviors when the ineffective behaviors are not working, and respond to cues in the environment that either support or refute your action—abilities critical to understanding violent behavior.

Diagnostic Considerations. Inmates are admitted to the California Psychiatric Program because some official has determined that they experience a mental disorder. *The Diagnostic and Statistical Manual-IV* (DSM-IV) defines a mental disorder as a "clinically significant behavioral or psychological syndrome or pattern that occurs in an individual and that is associated with present distress . . . or disability . . . or with a significantly increased risk of suffering death, pain, disability, or an important loss of freedom" (American Psychiatric Association, 1994). In the program, mental disorders are classified as psychotic, mood, psychotic and mood, or "organic."

Most, but not all, inmates who are admitted to the program are discharged with a diagnosis of a major mental disorder. Using only the primary mental disorder diagnosis, 30 percent are diagnosed with a psychotic disorder (schizophrenia, psychosis), 20 percent with a mood disorder (major depression, bipolar disorder), and 14 percent with a psychotic and mood disorder (schizoaffective, mood disorder with psychosis). Although 76 percent are discharged with a diagnosis of major mental disorder, 24 percent are discharged from the program without a diagnosis of major mental disorder. These inmates are diagnosed with malingering, no diagnosis on Axis I, or adjustment disorder.

Many, but not all, inmates also experience a personality disorder. Personality disorder is defined as "an enduring pattern of . . . behavior that deviates markedly from the expectations of the individual's culture, is pervasive and inflexible, has an onset in adolescence or early adulthood, is stable over time, and leads to distress or impairment" (American Psychiatric Association, 1994). Antisocial personality disorder, borderline personality disorder, and narcissistic personality disorder are the most frequently diagnosed disorders for this group of inmates. Although not currently included as a personality disorder in DSM-IV, psychopathy also is important in understanding this population.

Antisocial Personality Disorder. This disorder is a pattern of disregard for, and violation of, the rights of others. It is not a particularly relevant descriptor in trying to identify prisoners who are—or are not—violent because of the high prevalence of antisocial personality disorder among prisoners. Although the incidence of antisocial personality disorder in the general population is low (3 percent for males), the incidence in most prisons is approximately 75 percent. In this research sample, the incidence of antisocial personality disorder was 74 percent. Living a life that disregards the rights of others does not, however, in itself predict violence either in the community or in prison. In our sample, 61 percent of inmates with low violence were diagnosed with antisocial personality disorder, and 69 percent of inmates with high violence were diagnosed with antisocial personality disorder.

Borderline Personality Disorder. This is a pattern of instability in interpersonal relationships, self-image, and affects, and marked impulsivity. Inmates who experience borderline personality disorder often have long histories of various types of suicide gestures including cutting on themselves. Approximately 16 percent of our sample was diagnosed with borderline personality disorder. Borderline personality disorder, in contrast to antisocial personality disorder, is associated with violence, and inmates who were diagnosed with borderline personality disorder were 2.9 times more likely to be violent in prison and were 2.9 more likely to be violent in prison psychiatric treatment.

Narcissistic Personality Disorder. This is a pattern of grandiosity, need for admiration, and lack of empathy. Inmates who experience narcissistic personality disorder also frequently have a history of suicide gestures, but they do not have a history of the self-mutilation demonstrated by inmates with borderline personality disorder. The importance of narcissistic personality disorder in understanding violence in prison is the relationship between narcissistic traits and psychopathy.

Psychopathy. Psychopathy is not included in the DSM-IV, or any other DSM versions. Psychopathy, however, truly exists. And, in our research and the research of others, psychopathy plays a critical role in understanding violence. Psychopathy is characterized by two factors—antisocial lifestyle and selfish, callous, remorseless use of others. It is the "selfish, callous, remorseless use of others" that predicts violence (Hare, 1991). As previously indicated, the incidence of antisocial personality disorder in most prisons is approximately 75 percent, and in our sample it was 74 percent. The incidence of psychopathy, however, is much lower—18 to 22 percent in most prisons and 26 percent in our sample. That 26 percent of inmates, however, is responsible for an inordinate incidence of violence.

The scope of this chapter is not to focus on psychopathy, and we refer you to the work of Hare (1991) and Cleckley (1982) for further understanding of psychopathy. It also is not the focus of this chapter to introduce methods of diagnosing psychopathy. This evaluation should be done only by trained clinicians. Correctional staff who deal with inmates, however, should have some understanding of the construct. Increasingly, researchers are reporting a significant relationship between psychopathy and violence. One study looked at the relationship between psychopathy and violent recidivism. In this study (Rice, 1997), a retrospective review of treatment records of 292 Canadian inmates was conducted, and researchers identified twelve predictors to violent recidivism. Of these predictors, psychopathy was the most powerful predictor.

In one of our studies (Young, Justice, and Erdberg, 1999), we reported that inmates who are psychopathic are 6.7 times more likely to have a history of high violence. We also reported that psychopathic inmates are 3.5 to 8.3 times more likely to be violent in prison, and 2.4 to 4.8 times more likely to be violent in prison psychiatric treatment. All of this points to the reasonable assumption that psychopathy is likely overrepresented in supermax facilities. Therefore, we suggest that individuals working in supermax facilities be trained to understand this construct.

Specific Characteristics of Inmates Admitted from Supermax Facilities

Inmates throughout the state of California are referred to the psychiatric program, including inmates from California's supermax facilities. At this point in the project, 21 percent of the inmates in the research project have been admitted to the program from supermax facilities. Although similar in many ways, these "supermax inmates" differ from the rest of the sample in many ways. Supermax inmates were more likely to:

- be psychopathic
- have used drugs other than alcohol/marijuana first
- been highly violent in the community
- have a murder offense
- have more serious prison disciplinary actions
- have a lower ability to read
- have more impaired neuropsychological functioning for attention and concentration, memory and learning, and executive functioning

We think that the information this research provides is beneficial in understanding significant characteristics of a special population such as may be found in most supermax institutions. This understanding is necessary in developing programs to manage violence, and ultimately to have some impact on preventing future violence.

Program and Management Recommendations

It is our position that reducing violence in an institution need not be incompatible with reducing the potential for postrelease violence in the community. This section will focus on recommendations for management and treatment interventions that address both of these goals. Before discussing specific recommendations, we must acknowledge the parameters that are unique to supermax facilities. Many of these restrict or preclude implementation of some of the programs or interventions that have demonstrated success in reducing recidivism. Others may be feasible but at too great a risk of compromising security within the facility. All recommendations must be evaluated with respect to the specific institution, and within the context of physical, monetary, and legal constraints, all of which vary among facilities, across correctional departments.

One of the most common characteristics of supermax facilities is the restricted physical contact opportunities, imposed by physical design and operational policies. Again, these constraints vary considerably, with some supermax facilities having a range of internal security levels, and others being more singularly focused. Less than one-third of supermax facilities offer an opportunity for physical contact with staff. Several supermax facilities provide out-of-cell programming for individuals who have earned less restrictive confinement. These programs range from work and educational assignments to structured groups, but overall, such facilities are the exception. Opportunity for implementation of treatment programs will vary from facility to facility. Therefore, it is not the intent of this chapter to provide a blueprint for program implementation. The general recommendations that follow may constitute components of programs designed for a specific facility or interventions that may be used variably, in the day-to-day operation. The essential prerequisite to these recommendations must be staff training. Since most correctional facilities maintain comprehensive orientation and training programs, incorporation of treatment techniques is not unrealistic. The level and extent of training would need to be commensurate with the level of treatment planned.

Recommendations

First, we offer some recommendations specifically derived from the research described earlier. Then, we will broaden the perspective with contributions from other literature pertaining to effective treatment in prisons. Research in corrections has now reached the point where pragmatic applications can be supported and guided.

The following measures have been derived from the California psychiatric program research that characterizes men who were in supermax placement. Using these measures as a guide, we have made suggestions for interventions.

Young Age, Low Education, Low Socioeconomic Status, and Ethnic Diversity. Men who are in prison, and men who are in supermax facilities are young (average age is thirty-

three years), poorly educated (average education is tenth grade), from the lowest of socioeconomic groups (93-95 percent in the lowest socioeconomic groups), and predominantly non-Caucasian (79 percent). Within the confines of maintaining safety and security, interventions that are probably already in place which address physical activity, education, and work training might be relevant in reducing violence. Twenty-four percent of the men in the entire sample, and 36 percent of men in the supermax sample, had a life or life without parole sentence. Even for those men who would be spending the rest of their lives in prison, there needs to be some reason not to be violent. Finding a "place" in prison, or otherwise being able to earn some sort of privileges may play an important role in reinforcing nonviolent behaviors.

We fully recognize the difficulties in recruiting an ethnically diverse staff. Although we recognize that it is not a "new" suggestion, when culturally diverse staff is not available, the next best thing would be continuous training in cultural awareness and recognition of cultural differences.

Mental Illness or "Badness." As we discussed earlier, there is substantial evidence to support the conclusion that today's prisons, including today's supermax prisons, have become the mental hospitals of the past. Some, if not many, of these mentally ill men will wind up in supermax placement. There also is substantial evidence that individuals who are mentally ill, specifically inmates who are psychotic or schizophrenic, are more likely to be violent (Young, Justice, and Erdberg, 1999; Monahan, 1992; Helzer, Burnam, and McEvoy , 1991; Keith, Reiger, and Rae,1991). Identifying those inmates in supermax placement who are delusional, hallucinating, withdrawn, disorganized, and labeled by other inmates as "crazies" is certainly a first step in reducing violence in prison. Often, once appropriately medicated, these same inmates function adequately and nonviolently in the confines of prison. When they are not identified, and not appropriately medicated, however, these inmates are set up to be violent against others or the object of violence by others. Training that helps correctional personnel identify and distinguish signs and symptoms of mental illness from "badness" in the long run would be helpful in reducing violence.

Personality Disorders. Not all mental illness is schizophrenia, psychosis, or depression. Men who experience severe personality disorders (borderline personality disorder, narcissistic personality disorder, paranoid personality disorder) tend to "dip" into episodes of mental illness. Although often brief, these episodes of psychosis or depression can be severe, resulting in serious self-mutilation, hanging, jumping from tiers, or violently attacking officers and inmates. In addition to being aware of the signs and symptoms of major mental disorders, officers also need to be aware of the signs and symptoms of the primitive personality disorders. Being able to recognize an otherwise "sane" man who is dipping into a borderline or paranoid decompensation can go a long way towards preventing violence towards officers, other inmates, and the inmate himself.

Psychopathy. This construct was previously introduced in describing the characteristics of the research sample. Psychopathy is a well-known but complex constellation of behaviors that are characterized by a persistent antisocial lifestyle and pervasive grandiosity, callousness, and lack of empathy and remorse. Diagnosing psychopathy is a difficult process requiring specific training and experience that would not be expected of correctional personnel. Some psychopathic traits, however, are evident and identifiable.

Consideration of the type of disciplinary offenses committed by inmates provides one important piece of information in identifying the psychopathic inmate. Violence can be affective, or violence can be predatory. Affective violence occurs when the individual responds to a situation with obvious emotional reaction. Something happens, and the individual responds in a violent way. They often show signs of affect—increased heart beat, shallow breath, and perspiration.

Predatory violence, however, occurs when an individual simply acts—often without any particular situation that would likely cause that action. Predatory violence shows no signs of affect—but rather is cool, careful, planned, and without any observable signs of affect. Psychopathy and predatory violence go hand in hand. Unfortunately, at least in our sample, a preponderance of those inmates already identified as violent and placed in a supermax facility because of that violence were also psychopathic.

When not violent, however, these same individuals can be "charming," and manipulate even the most "seasoned" correctional officer into uncharacteristic actions. Being aware of the two-sided face of charm and predatory violence will go a long way to help staff anticipate violence. Correctional officials help should not be expected to diagnose psychopathy. Correctional officers, however, could be trained in identifying the constellations of traits that help to identify psychopaths.

Drug Abuse. Identifying inmates who abuse drugs is not a very sensitive discriminator of potential violence. In our sample, 90 percent of the inmates abused drugs, and 87 percent were polysubstance abusers. However, some patterns of drug use may be helpful in identifying potentially violent supermax offenders. In our sample, those inmates who used drugs other than alcohol and/or marijuana were more likely to be violent in prison. Inmates who used amphetamine, cocaine, PCP, LSD, heroin, and drugs other than alcohol/marijuana first were more likely to be in supermax placement, and more likely to be violent in prison. However, because drug abuse played a role in 90 percent of inmates' lives, drug abuse is a factor that should not be ignored. Drug abuse alone, though, did not get most of the inmates in our sample into prison. Nevertheless, drug abuse played a role in the lives and violence of 90 percent of the inmates in our sample.

Continued drug abuse treatment, drug screening, and drug education would address a need of most inmates in supermax placement. One model does not fit all inmates. Some inmates respond to the Alcoholics Anonymous/Narcotics Anonymous mode. Others respond to a relapse prevention model. Others respond to a cognitive-behavioral model. Whatever the model, exposure to drug treatment needs to be a part of the prison experience.

Current Offense. Many of the inmates in our sample had a history of assault (49 percent) in the community. For inmates in supermax placement, however, assault went further than assault, and predominantly included murder. Thirty-nine percent of inmates in supermax placement were in prison because of either murder or murder with special circumstances. Length of time in prison and length of prison sentence did not seem to make a difference. Committing murder did make a difference. Knowledge of the inmate's offenses would be one important piece of information for correctional officials to know.

Distinguishing the Level of Neuropsychological Functioning. Although some inmates in the sample demonstrated higher intellectual functioning, most inmates demonstrated intellectual functioning in the low average range. This pattern was demonstrated by inmates who were, and who were not, in supermax placement; therefore, "IQ" was not a discriminatory factor linked with violence. Inmates who were in supermax placement, however, were significantly more impaired on tests of "executive functioning." As previously indicated, executive functioning is the ability to think, reason, think ahead, anticipate consequences of actions before acting, problem solve, and find alternate ways of solving a problem. Inmates who were in supermax placement were significantly more likely to be impaired in these abilities. This is a group of men who cannot think ahead; cannot find different ways of dealing with their annoyances, cannot maintain their impulses, cannot anticipate the consequences of their actions; and often cannot stop their actions once those actions are put into motion. These problems are exacerbated and complicated by further

deficits in comprehension and cognitive processing. This results in difficulty comprehending and processing information, whether written or verbal and in reasoning out solutions to problems. This means that they are often unable to make relevant decisions, especially in circumstances which require immediate response. In such cases, violence may be the default response.

The causes for this impairment are speculative, though the data offers some significant contributors. The majority of the subjects in the sample experienced some type of head trauma. The high incidence of polysubstance abuse is also a possible contributor. The high use of inhalants, especially at the young age when they were typically first used and when brain structures are in early formative stages and highly vulnerable, may play a role. Whatever the causes, the pervasiveness of this impairment is a primary characteristic of the research sample, and is likely representative of a significant proportion of any supermax population.

Functionally, such cognitive limitations can impact all aspects of daily life. The potential for misinterpreting information is high. Superficially, these impairments are often not readily apparent. Many have compensated for these deficits by masking them with a façade of formidability, and many exhibit "street smarts" that suggest more intact cognitive ability than exists. Some individuals become very defensive when they are faced with situations that require cognitive functioning beyond their capabilities. They quickly resort to aggressive responses that have been long established and maintained (primarily through negative reinforcement) and are components of limited coping repertoires. The common adage "think before acting" is important here. Many lack the ability to do this. Thinking, if it occurs at all, is often retrospective, after acting rather than before. Impulsive behavior, whether threatening or violent, is often an early and frequent response simply because the individual possesses so few alternative options. Unfortunately, such responses have likely been at least sometimes effective in the past, and this firmly establishes them in the repertoire. Many preincarceration environments and many prison yards constitute situational contexts that specifically reinforce and strengthen these types of behavior patterns. In such social contexts, impulsivity and violence, often far exceeding what is sufficient in a given situation, becomes admired and praised. Social learning processes facilitate widespread adoption of such response patterns.

Closely related to the problem of cognitive deficits is the problem of immediate gratification. This phenomenon is not necessarily a direct result of cognitive impairment but is closely associated, and to some extent, maintained by it. Cognitive mediation supports delaying gratification, whether goal achievement or relief from stress. An individual knows, and tells himself that the circumstances of a given situation will change in time. Anxiety, for example, will pass as provoking contingencies change as may a real or perceived threat.

More importantly, taking the time to consider various responses usually results in a better choice. Again, the limitations in cognitive processing, along with a limited coping repertoire, complicate this important type of thinking. Individuals who function at this level are often unable to delay gratification, whether it is goal attainment, or eliminating a stressor. Internal controls are weak and inadequate. Impulsive behavior is reinforced because, despite its inappropriateness, it serves to immediately diminish the stressor, or the threat, even if only temporarily. That the long-term affect is disproportionately negative is not considered. The immediate situation consumes the available cognitive resources. Consequences of the response are at best perceived as a distant and vague possibility. Combine that precept with the fact that negative consequences may not occur at all, and the maladaptive response pattern becomes increasingly durable.

The big question remains: How can correctional staff more effectively manage these problems? Correctional staff can be educated in recognizing manifestations of cognitive impairment, especially when it is not readily apparent and may be easily attributable to volitional opposition or defiance. Understanding these deficits will provide correctional officers with the ability to deal with them on a day-to-day basis, in situations that often constitute high risk for violent behavior. Communication is a primary area. Correctional staff should be aware that inmate noncompliance with verbal instructions may be volitional opposition, or it may be due to poor comprehension. The inmate may respond to subsequent confrontation of noncompliance with a reactive defensiveness, including associated negative behaviors, rather than acknowledging or admitting his confusion. Clear and concise communication, as basic as it is, can negate otherwise escalating behaviors that may lead to violence. Beyond direct communication, per se, correctional staff should be aware that they influence inmates simply by being present. One factor that increases criminal behavior is the consistent association with criminals and lack of association with noncriminals. Correctional staff should be aware that they represent the only noncriminal social interactions inmates may receive, and act accordingly. Their actions, in terms of fairness, reason, and consistency, can provide very valuable nonverbal communication.

Further Recommendations

We have tried to identify empirically derived factors which may facilitate reducing violence by approaches and understanding that can be utilized on a day-to-day basis. Such improvement is contingent upon staff education and training in characteristics associated with violent behavior. We believe that the ultimate commitment to reducing violence in supermax, and later in the community, is the formal implementation of treatment programs aimed at reducing recidivism. This is a formidable goal for a correctional system, and one influenced by philosophy, mission, and probably most importantly, funding. As was discussed earlier, however, trends toward treatment in prison are increasing, predicated upon empirically demonstrated efficacy. Toward that end, the remainder of this chapter will focus on three elements that are associated with successful treatment programs in prison, again, as derived from recent research.

Organizational Commitment. Even more than providing funding, an institution which intends to implement a treatment program must have and demonstrate resolution and commitment to the process. Programs based primarily on rhetoric without substance waste resources, and cast doubt and suspicion on similar programs. The institution's administration must communicate this commitment as part of its mission. Such communication must be continual and consistent through program design and implementation. It must be part of new staff orientation, and ongoing training. Program effectiveness is dependent upon all staff recognizing that treatment is part of their responsibility and a performance expectation. Treatment programs cannot be conducted in a vacuum. Probably more than any other single factor, organizational commitment is critical to program success.

Understanding the Characteristics of the Inmate Population. This is the first step in designing a treatment program. To date there is a limited, but growing, body of research describing inmate populations which may be representative. Ideally, formal research describing the population may be sponsored by the institutions.

Characteristics often constitute targets for change themselves (substance abuse patterns), or as factors which require special accommodations in treatment and ongoing management (cognitive deficits). Once the characteristics of the treatment population are known, staff training must be undertaken. This is an essential component for effective treatment. Treatment must not be thought of as an isolated entity and assumed the only the purview of clinicians. In fact, it is correctional staff who have the greatest influence on inmates, and it is the generalization of therapeutic concepts to daily functioning which determine their ultimate benefit. Correctional staff must support and participate in the treatment process, and they can do so only by understanding the inmates and the treatment program. We hasten to qualify this reference to understanding, as this should not be interpreted as derogating the experiential understanding that correctional staff have acquired by their daily association with the inmate population. In most cases, empirical knowledge collaborates with experiential knowledge, and serves to enhance it. Ideally, it is an integration of the two that result in the most accurate picture and contributes to the most pragmatic application of knowledge to practice.

Cognitive Behavioral Approaches. A frequently demonstrated characteristic of successful prison programs (for example, those demonstrated to reduce recidivism) over the past two decades has been the use of cognitive behavioral approaches as opposed to psychodynamic models. Essentially, cognitive approaches focus on changing maladaptive patterns of thinking that lead to negative emotional states, and ultimately undesirable behavior. A wealth of resource material is available in this area (*see* especially Elliott and Verdeyen, 2003).

Cognitive therapy, provided in individual sessions or groups, conducted by credentialed clinicians offers high effectiveness. Thus far, this model offers the highest likelihood for generalization of therapeutic gains after returning to the community. Undoubtedly, the highest efficacy is achieved with comprehensive release planning and community follow up as a condition of parole. While community programs are beyond the scope of this chapter, the programs initiated and conducted in the facility are the key element in developing change and self-control ability. Cognitive therapy approaches, such as cognitive restructuring, are designed to change dysfunctional patterns of thinking, and to develop alternative ways of responding, particularly in high-risk situations.

The major disadvantage of cognitive therapy is the reliance on the functioning ability of the inmate. This is a major problem in many inmate populations that may limit the benefits of these programs. Therefore, therapy must be provided at a level consistent with the cognitive resources of the inmates. Some approaches may be very elementary with modest expectations. Some may be designed to capitalize on the greater cognitive abilities of higher-functioning inmates.

Unfortunately, for some inmates, cognitive functioning may be so compromised as to preclude acquiring all but the most basic coping skills, and in such cases, the only option is the ongoing provision of high levels of structure and external control. In the California psychiatric treatment program, two levels of cognitive groups are provided, addressing lower and higher functioning levels of inmate participants. Another disadvantage of most cognitive therapy approaches is the reliance on the participant's motivation. Inmates who do not apply themselves will not benefit. Initial involvement in therapy can be enhanced with positive reinforcement by earning privileges based on progress. It is our experience that initially, the opportunity for therapy is often an incentive in itself, in that attendance allows time out of cells. As therapy continues, the progress made, particularly as verbally reinforced by a therapist, becomes a self-sustaining factor. Often immediate benefits are seen in institutional behavior management. Time spent productively reduces time spent in problematic ways.

Implementing and maintaining therapeutic approaches such as those suggested offers potential value in ultimately protecting society by decreasing the likelihood of violence after release. Therapeutic approaches offer immediate institutional value because they occupy inmates in productive endeavors and provide immediate and tangible reinforcement, thereby reducing negative attitudes and antagonistic behaviors. Most important, as inmates acquire coping skills, the benefits become apparent in all functioning areas. Implementing evidence-based treatment allows prisons to provide societal protection not only by incarcerating the offenders but also by helping offenders make minor or significant changes in their behavior. It is this latter opportunity that offers the greatest benefit to society.

Summary

In this chapter, we have discussed several factors relevant to understanding violence in a supermax facility. We have discussed violence in society, the changing prevalence of violence, and possible explanations for these changes. We also have discussed violence in prison, and consequently the need and justification for supermax facilities. And we have discussed changes in correctional policy from the focus on "rehabilitation" to the focus on "punishment."

We discussed the results of a research project conducted within a California prison psychiatric program describing characteristics of inmates in supermax facilities. Based on this research, we suggested recommendations for managing violence in supermax facilities. These suggestions include recognition of the young age and long prison sentences of many supermax inmates; recognition of the cultural diversity of supermax inmates; recognition of the likely prevalence of mental illness among supermax inmates; the need to discriminate between mental illness and "badness;" recognition of the role of drug use among supermax inmates; and recognition of the prevalence of brain damage and cognitive impairments among supermax inmates.

We discussed broadening these suggestions beyond research findings including the need for appropriate risk assessment, an empirical description of inmates, and recognition not only of cognitive limitations but also coping limitations; and the need for immediate gratification of needs. We discussed the effectiveness of applying principles of behavioral and cognitive-behavioral approaches to the supermax setting.

We have a number of suggestions based on our research, and the research of others. What we do not have is research demonstrating the effectiveness of these suggestions in supermax populations. Our hope is that this information, or some part of this information, is useful for the management of violence within supermax facilities, and in lessening, if even incrementally, the likelihood of future violence in the community.

NOTES

[1] Information in this chapter reflects the opinions of the authors, and the authors assume responsibility for all opinions provided. Information may, nor may not, reflect the opinions of the California Department of Mental Health and/or the psychiatric program from which data was obtained.

REFERENCES

American Psychiatric Association. 1994. *Diagnostic and Statistical Manual of Mental Disorders, 4th ed., rev.* Washington, D.C.: American Psychiatric Association.

Andrews, D. and J. Bonta. 1994. *The Psychology of Criminal Conduct.* Cincinnati, Ohio: Anderson Press.

Beck, A. 2000. *State and Federal Prisoners Returning to the Community: Findings from the Bureau of Justice Statistics.* Keynote address at the First Reentry Courts Initiative Cluster Meeting, Washington D.C.

Bureau of Justice Statistics. 2000. *Correctional Populations in the United States.* Washington, D.C.: Bureau of Justice Statistics.

Cleckley, H. 1982. *The Mask of Insanity.* New York: New American Library.

Elliott, B. and V. Verdeyen. 2003. *Game Over: Strategies for Redirecting Inmate Deception.* Lanham, Maryland: American Correctional Association.

Evans, D. 1996. *Current Trends in Violence.* Keynote address presented at the National Symposium on Violent Offenders, Washington, D.C.

Gendreau, P. 1996. *Offender Rehabilitation: What We Know and What Needs to Be Done.* Criminal Justice and Behavior. 23(1): 144-161.

Gendreau, P., T. Little, and C. Goggin. 1995. *A Meta-analysis of the Predictors of Assault Offender Recidivism: Assessment Guidelines for Classification and Treatment.* Ottawa, Canada: Ministry Secretariat Solicitor General of Canada.

Hare, R. D. 1991. *The Hare Psychopoathy Checklist-Revised Manual.* North Tonawanda, New York: Multi-Health Systems.

Helzer, J., A. Burnam, and L. McEvoy. 1991. Alcohol Abuse and Dependence. In L. M. Robbins and D. A. Reiger, eds. *Psychiatric Disorders in America: The Epidemiologic Catchment Area Study.* New York: Free Press.

Keith, S., D. Reiger, and D. Rae. 1991. Schizophrenic Disorders. In L. M. Robbins and D.A. Reiger, eds. *Psychiatric Disorders in America: The Epidemiologic Catchment Area Study.* New York: Free Press.

Lipton, D., R. Martinson, and J. Wilks. 1975. *The Effectiveness of Correctional Treatment: A Survey of Treatment Evaluation Studies.* New York: Praeger Press.

Monahan, J. 1992. Mental Disorder and Violent Behavior. *American Psychologist.* 47(4): v, 584-589.

Myers, J. K. and L. Bean. 1968. *A Decade Later: A Follow-Up of Social Class and Mental Illness.* New York: John Wiley and Sons.

National Commission on the Causes and Prevention of Violence. 1969. *To Establish Justice, To Ensure Domestic Tranquility.* Washington, D.C.: U.S. Government Printing Office.

U.S. Department of Justice. 1997. *Supermax Housing: A Survey of Current Practice.* Longmont, Colorado: National Institute of Corrections Information Center.

Young, M., J. Justice, and P. Erdberg. 1999. Risk Factors for Violent Behavior among Incarcerated Male Psychiatric Patients: A Multimethod Approach. *Assessment.* 6(3): 243-258.

The Ohio State Penitentiary is Ohio's only high maximum-security facility. It was completed in April 1998 to house Ohio's most serious, predatory, and violent adult male inmates. *Photo courtesy of the Ohio Department of Rehabilitation and Correction.*

The largest of the three buildings of the Ohio State Penitentiary is the Penitentiary itself, which is a covered design that encompasses approximately 340,000 square feet. *Photo courtesy of the Ohio Department of Rehabilitation and Correction.*

The entire Ohio State Penitentiary Complex is situated on a 240-acre tract of land. Both the Penitentiary and the Correctional Camp (a separate minimum-security camp) are equipped with paved perimeter roads, which are patrolled twenty-four hours per day, seven days per week. *Photo courtesy of the Ohio Department of Rehabilitation and Correction.*

A single no-climb fence equipped with microwave detection and a perimeter detection system surrounds the Ohio State Penitentiary. *Photo courtesy of the Ohio Department of Rehabilitation and Correction.*

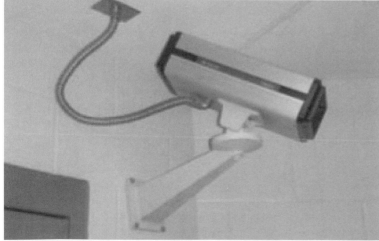

Security measures at the Ohio State Penitentiary include restrictive inmate movement, single cells, and security cameras throughout the penitentiary. These allow officers to monitor virtually all areas. *Photo courtesy of the Ohio Department of Rehabilitation and Correction.*

All housing areas of the Ohio State Penitentiary are equipped with state-of-the-art computerized electronically controlled pods and security cameras. *Photo courtesy of the Ohio Department of Rehabilitation and Correction.*

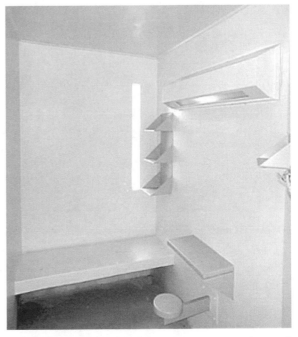

The Colorado State Penitentiary consists of four separate housing units each containing 126 single-person cells per unit for a total of 504 cells. Sixteen of these cells are handicapped accessible. *Photo courtesy of Lt. Steve Paolino, Colorado State Penitentiary.*

The Colorado State Penitentiary pictured here was the prototype for the design of the Ohio State Penitentiary. *Photo courtesy of Lt. Steve Paolino, Colorado State Penitentiary.*

Two correctional officers escort an inmate to the shower at the Colorado State Penitentiary. *Photo courtesy of Lt. Steve Paolino, Colorado State Penitentiary.*

The dayhall of the Colorado State Penitentiary shows the two-tiered arrangement of cells. *Photo courtesy of Lt. Steve Paolino, Colorado State Penitentiary.*

About the Authors

Donice Neal, the editor and one of the authors of this volume, received her bachelor of arts degree from Adams State College in 1971 with a major in psychology and minors in sociology and music. Following graduation, she worked as a case worker for social services for a small rural county in Colorado. She returned to school attending Trinity University in San Antonio, Texas, where she received a master of science in psychology with a clinical specialization. Warden Neal worked as a school psychologist and in private practice after completing graduate school. She began her career in corrections in 1979 when she began working as a psychologist for Colorado's Division of Rehabilitation. In 1983, she began working directly for the Colorado Department of Corrections as a correctional specialist at the Reception and Diagnostic Center (RDC) in Canon City. She was promoted to manager of the RDC in 1986 and to deputy warden at the Colorado Women's Correctional Facility (CWCF) in 1988. In 1990, she became warden of CWCF. Since that time she has been the warden of four facilities including the Colorado State Penitentiary when it opened in 1993. Warden Neal is currently assigned as the warden of the Canon Minimum Centers. The Minimum Centers consist of three minimum and minimum restricted facilities, Skyline Correctional Center, Four Mile Correctional Center, and Arrowhead Correctional Center, located on a 6,000 acre complex in Canon City.

Eugene E. Atherton is the assistant director of prisons of the western region in the Colorado Department of Corrections. He was a warden at Colorado State Penitentiary, a level 5 security administrative segregation facility. Its mission is to provide a highly specialized approach of simultaneously isolating Colorado's most high-risk inmates and preparing them for parole, discharge, or return to the general population. The Colorado State Penitentiary was the first "supermax" facility to receive American Correctional Association accreditation and special recognition of the ACA Best Practices award in 1998. Prior to this, he has been a case manager, an operations lieutenant, a housing captain, a security major, housing manager, security specialist, warden, and chief of security for the Colorado Department of Corrections. For many years, he has served as a consultant and trainer on special projects for the National Institute of Corrections, and as an expert witness in legal proceedings at the federal level. He is the coauthor of the American Correctional Association book, *Use of Force: Current Policy and Practice* and contributing editor for the ACA book, *Guidelines for the Development of a Security Program*. He received his bachelor of arts degree in social science with an emphasis on personnel management and industrial/labor relations from Michigan State University.

James H. Bruton has more than thirty-four years' experience in corrections. He retired as warden from the Oak Heights Minnesota Correctional Facility, the state's maximum-security prison. Prior to this, he served as deputy commissioner in the institutions division of the Minnesota Department of Corrections. He is an adjunct faculty member at several schools: the University of St. Thomas Criminal Justice Department, the University of Minnesota Sociology Department, Hamline University Sociology Department, and Minneapolis Community College. He holds a master of art degree from the College of St. Thomas and a bachelor of science degree from the University of Minnesota. He is also the author of a book on prisons to be published in 2004 (Voyageur Press).

Gregory A. Bucholtz is an assistant chief inspector and formerly research administrator for the Ohio Department of Rehabilitation and Correction. Dr. Bucholtz earned his Ph.D. from the University of Louisville in urban and public affairs. He is also an adjunct faculty member in the Department of Sociology at the Ohio State University, teaching in the areas of crime and delinquency, research methods and statistics, and policing.

Before his retirement, after twenty-eight years in correctional service, **James M. Greco** was the executive associate warden of ADX Florence, and prior to that, he held the same position at U.S. Penitentary Florence, in Florence, Colorado. During his career, he served more than twenty-five years with the Federal Bureau of Prisons. He earned his bachelor of arts degree in sociology and speech from Northwestern Oklahoma State University and his master of arts in criminal justice administration from Oklahoma City University. After serving in the U.S. Marine Corps, he was commissioned in the U.S. Army reserves and retired as lieutenant colonel in 2002. Currently, he is a staff leader/instructor at the U.S. Army's Command and General Staff College, Combined Arms and Services Staff School at Fort Leavenworth, Kansas.

James D. Hart is the associate warden for treatment at Dodge Correctional Institution, a maximum-security facility, where he is responsible for coordination of assessment and evaluation, clinical, dental and medical evaluation, and record compilation for all new adult male inmates sentenced to Wisconsin correctional institutions. He

received both his masters of science in social work and his bachelor of arts in psychology from the University of Wisconsin-Madison. He is past president of Corrections Ministries of Wisconsin and is currently a member of the Parole Commission in the state of Wisconsin.

Jerald Justice is a program consultant for the California Department of Mental Health, Vacaville Psychiatric Program. This entails conducting an ongoing evaluation of the effectiveness of the hospital's programs and conducting research projects to describe the patient population. He oversees the Psychiatric Social Work Program and provides clinical supervision and consultation. He received his master of social work degree from Denver University, a master's degree in social science from the University of Northern Colorado, and a bachelor of science degree in sociology from the University of Southern Colorado. He is licensed as a clinical social worker.

Nolin Renfrow is the current director of prisons for the Colorado Department of Corrections. The director of prisons is responsible for the management and operations of all of Colorado's adult institutions. Mr. Renfrow began his corrections career in 1978 as a correctional officer. Working primarily in administrative segregation facilities, he was promoted through the ranks, becoming a warden in 1994. In 1997, Mr. Renfrow was promoted to the director of facilities management, where he is responsible for managing new construction, remodels, renovations, and controlled maintenance processes for all facilities. His duties also include preconstruction activities such as programming, design, and procurement/contracting activities. Mr. Renfrow's educational background includes a bachelor's degree in business administration, and he currently is in the process of obtaining a master's degree in public administration.

Thomas J. Stickrath is the assistant director of the Ohio Department of Rehabilitation and Correction. He is responsible for approximately 78,700 offenders in prisons, on parole, or in state-funded community sanctions, more than 15,000 employees, and a $1.4 billion annual budget. Prior to this, he was a warden at several Ohio institutions. He served on the Standards Committee of the American Correctional Association. Mr. Stickrath holds his juris doctorate degree in law and his bachelor of science in business administration from The Ohio State University.

Myla H. Young received a Ph.D. in psychology from the California Professional School of Psychology, Alameda, and has two years of post-doctoral training in neuropsychology at San Francisco General Hospital/ University of California, San Francisco. She is board certified in Neuropsychology (ABPN). Dr. Young currently serves as senior supervising psychologist and director of an American Psychological Association accredited psychology intern training program. Research interests and publications include neuropsychological functioning of inmates, risk factors for community and prison violence, risk factors for suicide and self-harm, cultural differences in psychiatrically hospitalized inmates, and psychopathy.

Index

A

access control systems, 61
adjacencies, 25
administration, see headings at management
Alcatraz, v, 3
American Correctional Association (ACA)
    staff training guidelines, 44
American Psychiatric Association, 105
antisocial personality disorder, 106, 109
architectural program plans, 21
assaults, inmate-on-staff, *see also* violence
    management research
    incentive-based programs, 92, 95, 96-97
    Ohio statistics, 1996-2000, 6-8
Atherton, Eugene E., 67-84, 119
Auburn, New York State Prison at, 2
audio-video cameras, 60-61

B

background checks and screening
    construction of facility, 24
    staff, 40
behavior of inmates
    deterrence factors, 11-12
    incentive-based programs, 85, 95-97
    reasons for admittance to supermax facil-
    ities, 2, 3-4, 5-6
Bell v. Wolfish, 68
biometrics, 61-62
borderline personality disorder, 106, 109
brain functioning and violence management
    research, 105, 110-11
Bruton, James H., 85-98, 119-20
Bucholtz, Gregory A., 1-14, 120
building supermax prisons, *see* construction
    of supermax prisons

C

California Psychiatric Program and Research
    Project, 103 *et seq.*
cameras and monitors
    audio and video cameras, 60-61, 94
    closed-circuit television, 59, 60
    deterrent function, 24, 25-26
    incentive-based programming, 94
    technological devices, 60-61
Canada, 100, 101
cells
    construction, 24-25
    forced entry, 73-74
    isolation in, 1-2, 8-10
    shakedowns, 92, 93
cellular phones, 58
characteristics of inmates, 103-7, 112
chemical nonlethal weapons, 64
closed-circuit television systems, 59, 60
cognitive behavioral approaches, 112-13
cognitive deficits and violent inmates, 105,
    110-11
Colorado
    Department of Corrections mission state-
    ment, 29, 30
    Florence, Administrative Maximum Peni-
    tentiary at, v, 3, 8, 10
    State Penitentiary, 91, 117
    Sterling Correctional Facility, 55
communications
    information management, 59-60
    perimeter security, 55
    security technology, 58-60
    staff training, 46-47, 89
    verbal direction as force option, 71
concentration/consolidation approach to
    high-risk inmates, 2, 3
conceptual design, 20
construction of supermax prisons, 15-27

costing and funding, 16-17
delivery strategies, 18, 22-23
design process, 17-22
goals, 19
illustrations, 116-17
inspections, 26
materials, 17, 25
need for, demonstrating, 15-16
programming, 16, 18, 19-21
security issues, 23-26
violent inmates, 101
contraband, 56-57, 91
cost issues, 16-17, 37
"crash lines," 59
cross-disciplinary approach, 34-36, 39
culture of workplace, 38-39, 49-51

D
dayhalls or pods, 24-25
decentralization/dispersal approach to high-
risk inmates, 2, 3, 8
delivery strategies, construction of supermax prisons, 18, 22-23
demographics of inmates, 104, 108
deployment of equipment, 75-76
depressive disorders, 9, 108-9
design process, 17-22
deterrence, 11-12, 24-26
Diagnostic and Statistical Manual-IV (DSM-IV),
105, 106
diagnostics, 105-7
Dickens, Charles, 1
direct supervision of officers, effect of, 71, 94
dispersal/decentralization approach to high-
risk inmates, 2, 3, 8
disruptive events
incentive-based programs, 95
staff training, 45, 46-47, 48-49
diversity of staff, 41-42
documentation of use of force, 83
"door warrior" mentality, 38, 39
doors, locking systems for, 57-58, 61
drug abuse, 105, 109-10
duress alarms, 58-59

E
Eastern State Penitentiary, 1, 2
educational programming, 85, 87, 89, 108
electronic nonlethal weapons, 64

emergencies
fires, 62-63
staffing, 46-47, 48-49, 65
use of force, 74, 75
emergency response teams (ERTs), 74
ethnic/racial diversity
inmates, 104, 108
staff, 41, 42, 108
excessive use of force, 48, 67-69, 76-78

F
false rejection rate (FRR) and false acceptance rate (FAR), biometric systems, 62
federal supermax prisons, v, 3, 29
female staff, 41-42
fences, 24, 54-55
fingerprint biometric systems, 62
fire safety, 62-63
Florence, CO, Administrative Maximum Penitentiary, v, 3, 8, 10
fluoroscopes, 57, 94
force, use of, *see* use of force
funding issues, 16-17, 37

G
gangs, 2, 5
goals, 29, 33-36
construction of supermax prisons, 19
defined, 30
incentive systems for inmates, 85
mission and mission statements, 29-33,
38, 45, 50
staff understanding of, 34-35, 38
Gondles, James A., v
Greco, James M., 37-51, 120

H
hand measurement biometric systems, 62
Hart, James D., 29-36, 120
Hudson v. McMillian, 69

I
Illinois, Marion USP, v, 3, 8
immediate gratification and impulsivity, 105,
106, 111
incentive systems, 10-11, 26, 85-98
assaults, inmate-on-staff, 92, 95, 96-97
behavioral issues, 85, 95-97
consequences and rewards, 95-96

disruptive events, 95
expulsion from, 96
goals, understanding, 34-35
long-term or no-release sentences, 87-88
mission and goals, 85
philosophy of, 85, 86-87
programming, 86-87, 88-89, 97-98
security issues, 91-97
social/public expectations, 87, 89
staff, 26, 86, 89-90
training, 89-90
violent inmates, 107-13
visiting privileges, 90-91
incidents, disruptive
incentive-based programs, 95
staff training, 45, 46-47, 48-49
information management, 59-60
infrastructure analyses, 17
inmates, *see also* more specific topics
characteristics of, 103-7, 112
goals, understanding, 34-35
long-term or life sentences, 87-88
mission and mission statement, awareness of, 32
rehabilitation, 102-3
work activities, 41
inspections
construction of supermax prisons, 26
technology systems, 66
institutional management issues, 3-5
intellectual functioning, 105, 110-11
intercom systems, 58-59
internal detection systems, 55-57
Interstate Compact Agreement, 2
interviewing potential staff, 41
intrusion detectors, 56
iris biometric systems, 62
isolation, 1-2, 8-10

J
Justice, Jerald, 99-115, 120

K
keys and locks, 57-58, 61

L
lethal fences, 24, 55
lethal force, 73
life, inmates likely to serve for, 87-88

light beam intrusion systems, 56
lockdowns, 91-92, 93, 95
locks and locking systems, 57-58, 61
long-term sentences, 87-88

M
Madrid v. Gomez, 68
maintenance, 66, 93
"management by walking around," 38-39
management, institutional, 3-5
management staff
development of workplace culture, 38
mission and goals, 31-33, 38
treatment programs, commitment to, 112
use of force, administrative oversight of, 78-79
Marion, IL, U.S. penitentiary in, v, 3, 8
mental health
California Psychiatric Program and Research Project, 103 et seq.
level of custody and, 8-10
violence management research findings, 103-7, 108-9
metal detectors, 94
Minnesota Multiphasic Personality Inventory (MMPI), 103
Minnesota's Oak Park Heights high-security prison, 89, 91, 95, 97
mission and mission statements, 29-33, 38, 45, 50, 85
monitoring and surveillance
audio and video cameras, 60-61, 94
closed-circuit television, 59, 60
deterrent function, 24, 25-26
incentive-based programming, 94
technological devices, 60-61
multidisciplinary approach, 34-36, 39
murder, inmates committing, 110

N
narcissistic personality disorder, 106, 109
National Commission on the Causes and Prevention of Violence (1969), 100
Neal, Donice, 53-66, 119
need for supermax facility, demonstrating, 15-16
neuropsychological functioning and violence management research, 105, 110-11
New York State Prison at Auburn, 2
nonlethal weapons, 63-64

125

O

Oak Park Heights, MN high-security prison, 89, 91, 95, 97

objectives, *see* goals

offense leading to imprisonment, nature of, 110

Ohio

    inmate-on-staff assaults, 1996-2000, 6-8

    Southern Ohio Correctional Facility, 5

Ohio State Penitentiary (OSP)

    approvals and denials of admittance, 7

    criteria for supermax placement, 3-4, 5

    illustrations, 116-17

    mental health issues, 10

    security levels, movement through, 10-11

Oleoresin Capsicum (OC), 73

operational program plans, 20-21

P

paranoid personality disorder, 109

pat searches, 94

Pennsylvania's Eastern State Penitentiary, 1, 2

perimeter security, 24, 54-55

personal alarms, 59

personality disorders of violent inmates, 106-7, 109

phone systems, 58-59

physical force, 72, *see also* use of force

pods or dayhalls, 24-25

predatory violence, 109

presence of officers, effect of, 71, 94

programming

    commitment to treatment programs, 112

    construction of supermax facilities, 16, 18, 19-21, 26

    educational, 85, 87, 89, 108

    goals, meshing with, 34-35

    incentive systems for inmates, 86-87, 88-89, 97-98

    requirement to participate in, 86-87

    specialized staff, 41

    staffing needs, 37

    violent inmates, recommendations for, 101-3, 107-13

psychopathy, 106-7, 109

Psychopathy Checklist (PCL-R), 103

psychosis, 108-9

public safety issues, 101-2

public sentiment and expectations, 13, 87, 89, 99-100, 102

Q

Quakers, 1

Quebec Long-Term Segregation Unit, 10

R

racial/ethnic diversity

    inmates, 104, 108

    staff, 41, 42, 108

recidivism reduction, 111-13

records of use of force, 83

Red Onion State Prison, VA, 2

rehabilitation, 102-3

release, inmates unlikely to obtain, 87-88

religious volunteers, 42-43

Renfrow, Nolin, 15-27, 120

repairs, 66, 93

request for qualifications/request for proposal (RFQ/RFP), 19

research in violence management, *see* violence management research

restraints, 73-74

retention of staff, 49-51

retinal biometric systems, 62

Rohrschach test, 103

S

scenario development, 20

schizophrenia, 108-9

screening and background checks

    construction of facility, 24

    staff, 40

searches, 94

security issues, *see also* specific devices

    committee on security technology, 55

    construction of supermax facilities, 23-26

    consultants, 24

    control of security information, 24

    goals of facility, 35-36

    incentive systems for inmates, 91-97

    layered security envelopes, 24-25

    operations as form of, 25

    reasons for supermax prisons, 5-8

    shakedowns, 92, 93

    staff, importance of, 23, 25-26, 60, 64-66, 94

    technology, *see* technology

testing systems, 65-66
tool control, 92-93
volunteers, 44
segregated units within prisons, 4-5, 6-8
services for inmates and construction of supermax prisons, 25
shakedowns, 92, 93
site analyses, 17
site lines, 25
"Smart Cards," 61
social control, 11-12
social/public expectations, 13, 87, 89, 99-100, 102
society, safety of, 101-2
society, violence in, 99-100
sociodemographics of inmates, 104, 108
solitary confinement, 1-2, 8-10
Southern Ohio Correctional Facility, 5
space requirements, determining, 19-20
spatial differentiation, effects of, 4-5
special tactical response teams, use of force by, 75
staff, 37-51
  communications skills, 46-47, 89
  direct supervision and presence, effect of, 71, 94
  diversity of workforce, 41, 42, 108
  experienced versus inexperienced correctional workers, 39-40, 46
  fire prevention skills, 63
  goals, understanding, 34-35, 38
  incentive systems, 26, 86, 89-90
  interviews, 41
  intrusion systems, 56
  managerial, see management staff
  mission and mission statement, 32, 38, 45, 50
  multidisciplinary approach, 34-36, 39
  nonlethal weapons training, 64
  perimeter security, 55
  programming needs, 37
  retention strategies, 49-51
  security technology committee, 55
  selection process, 39-42
  stress issues, 45, 48, 50, 70-71, 77
  technology and security, importance to, 23, 25-26, 60, 64-66, 94
  training, see training
  volunteers, 42-44

workplace culture and work ethic, 38-39, 49-51
state supermax prisons, v, 3
Sterling Correctional Facility, CO, 55
Stickrath, Thomas J., 1-14, 120-21
stress on staff, 45, 48, 50, 70-71, 77
supermax prisons, see also more specific topics
  definition of, 101
  federal, v, 3, 29
  historical background, v, 1, 2-3
  inmate population requiring, 101
  reasons for, 1-14, 101
  special characteristics of inmates, 107
  state, v, 3
surveillance, see monitoring and surveillance
SWAT and SORT teams, 75

T
tactical response teams, 75
teams for specialized use of force, 73-75
technology, 53-66, see also specific devices and systems
  committee on security technology, 55
  construction of supermax facilities, 25-26
  illustrations, 116-17
  repairs, maintenance, and inspections, 66
  staff, importance of, 23, 25-26, 60, 64-66, 94
  systems, 53-64
  testing systems, 65-66
  use of force, 83-84
telephones, 58-59
tool control, 92-93
tough-on-crime mindset, public sentiment supporting, 13, 87, 89, 99-100, 102
training, 38, 44-49, 65
  communications, 46-47, 89
  fire prevention skills, 63
  incentive systems for inmates, 89-90
  mental disorders of inmates, 108-9
  nonlethal weapons, 64
  security and technology, 65
  use of force, 38, 47-48, 70-71, 79-82
  volunteers, 42, 44
trend analysis, 16

U
United States, violence in, 100
use of force, 67-84
    administrative oversight systems, 78-79
    cell entry teams, 73-74
    criteria for appropriateness of, 69
    deployment of equipment, 75-76
    documentation, 83
    emergencies, 74, 75
    excessive use of force, 48, 67-69, 76-78
    legal issues, 67-69
    national survey Use of Force: Current Policy and Practice, 76, 78
    nonlethal weapons, 63-64
    philosophy and policy issues, 69-71, 82-83
    physical force, 72
    planned use of force, 75
    teams, 73-75
    technology, 83-84
    training, 38, 47-48, 70-71, 79-82
    types or options, 71-73, 81

V
verbal direction as force option, 71
video cameras, 60-61, 94
video conferencing, 59
violence management research, 99-115
    characteristics of inmates, 103-7, 112
    cognitive behavioral approaches, 112-13
    drug abuse, 105, 109-10
    mental condition and brain functioning, 103-7, 108-11
    offense, nature of, 110
    prison, violence in, 100-103
    programming recommendations, 101-3, 107-13
    rehabilitation, 102-3
    society, violence in, 99-100
    sociodemographics, 104, 108
    supermax facilities, 101-2
    supermax inmates, special characteristics of, 107
visiting privileges, 90-91
volunteer staff, 42-44

W
wardens, *see* management staff
Wilkinson, Reginald, v, 5
Wisconsin Department of Corrections

    mission statement, 29-30
women on staff, 41-42
workplace culture and work ethic, 38-39, 49-51

X
X-ray machines, 57

Y
Young, Myla A., 99-115, 121